FOLKS WHO TALK FUNNY

Down in North Carolina and North Georgia, a lot of Florida people have bought land and moved in at least for the summer. One fall, about October, a man from the North who had read the *Foxfire* books came down to meet first-hand some of the mountain people he had been reading about. He pulled into a service station for a fill-up and while he was there he inquired of the station attendant, "Where could I find some of these people who talk so funny?"

The attendant looked at him a minute and replied, "You're too late, they've all gone back to Florida for the winter."

LAUGHTER IN APPALACHIA

A Festival of Southern Mountain Humor

Loyal Jones and Billy Edd Wheeler

IVY BOOKS • NEW YORK

Ivy Books
Published by Ballantine Books
Copyright © 1987 by Billy Edd Wheeler and Loyal Jones

Library of Congress Catalog Card Number: 86-32263

ISBN 0-8041-0299-6

This edition published by arrangement with August House, Inc., Publishers

Printed in Canada

First Ballantine Books Edition: August 1988
Fourth Printing: June 1990

To all the belly-laughers, sly-winkers, jokesters,
prefabricated and home-grown humorists of
    Appalachia who
use humor and laughter to get them through life.

Contents

Preface

The compilers of this book have long used humor as a way of getting along and doing business in the world. We have noticed that people seem to crave a good laugh and that humor prepares a person, a small group, or a large audience for more serious matters. It catches their attention and puts them in a receptive frame of mind.

One of us (Wheeler) is a songwriter, playwright, poet, singer, and storyteller. The other (Jones) is a teacher, administrator, writer, and storyteller who makes frequent speeches. We both employ a great deal of humor in what we do. Consequently, we have collected jokes and stories over most of our lives.

A few years ago, we got together and came up with the idea of doing a book on Appalachian humor. Doubting that we had enough material in our own collections, we dreamed up a humor festival to which people would be invited to share their best stories and compete for prizes. With the help of the Kentucky Arts Council, the Kentucky Humanities Council, and Druthers International, we held a Festival of Appalachian Humor at Berea College on June 15–16, 1983. To insure a thoughtful look at humor, befitting a college, we invited two scholars of humor to participate: Dr. W. Gordon Ross, Professor Emeritus of Philosophy and Religion at Berea College, and Dr. Robert J. Higgs, Professor of English at East Tennessee State University. To guarantee robust humor, we invited a variety of regional humorists, most of them friends of ours: Joe Bly, Dr. Eslie Asbury, Bob Terrell, Connie Regan, Barbara Freeman, David Holt, Ernest "Doc" McConnell, and

Byron Crawford. All agreed that we could use some of their material, as did winners of prizes in several categories and the many contestants.

In addition, we invited friends to contribute one or two of their best stories. We have tried to credit all contributors, even some of those who told us stories years ago. We apologize for not giving credit to some whom we may have forgotten. We are grateful for these gifts, and we thank you. We have also asked to reprint stories from *Goldenseal: West Virginia Traditional Life*, a quarterly magazine of the West Virginia Department of Culture and History, and we especially want to thank Ken Sullivan and his contributors for permission to reprint this material. We also thank Betty Stephens Lamb, who transcribed hours of recordings, and Joan Kuyper, who typed the manuscript.

Good stories make the rounds and become the property of those who appreciate them and take the trouble to remember them. Therefore we invite you, the readers, to remember those that you like. If we missed a good one, and you are so inclined, send it along to us at one of the addresses below, and we just might begin another volume.

> *Billy Edd Wheeler*
> Box 7
> Swannanoa, NC 28778
>
> *Loyal Jones*
> Berea College,
> Box 2336
> Berea, KY 40404

Acknowledgments

Most of the jokes attributed to *Goldenseal* arose from the annual West Virginia State Liar's Contest. For more information on that event, write the Department of Culture and History, Capitol Complex, Charleston, WV 25305.

The editors cite the following jokes reprinted by permission from *Goldenseal*: Bonnie Collins, "A Dream About Hell," *Goldenseal* 9:1 (Spring, 1983), 68–69; Bonnie Collins, "Unsanitary Pork," *Goldenseal* 9:1 (Spring, 1983), 70; Riley Wilson, "Reach Me the Tin," *Goldenseal* 8:2 (Summer, 1982), 62–64; Bill Jeffries, "My Monkey's Your Monkey", *Goldenseal* 10:2 (Summer, 1984), 36-7; Bill Jeffries, "The Snakebit Hoe Handle," *Goldenseal* 10:2 (Summer, 1984), 36; Eric Waggoner, "You Can't Please Everybody," *Goldenseal* 11:1 (Spring, 1985), 71; and Nat Reese, "Uncle Ketchup and Aunt Tomato," *Goldenseal* 11:1 (Spring, 1985), 70–71.

"The Wheelchair Case," "The Skin Board," and "The Accordion Dog" appear in John M. Ramsay's *Dog Tales* (Kentucky Imprints, Berea, Kentucky 40403) and are reprinted here with permission of the author.

"In a Southerly Direction" is from *Out in the Country Back Home: Poems* by Jeff Daniel Marion (Winston-Salem: The Jackpine Press, 1976), and is reprinted here with permission of the publisher.

The material from the chapter "Jesse James Bailey" is used here with permission of Beau Buchanan.

It's Either Funny or It Ain't

BILLY EDD WHEELER

I love to laugh.

All my life I have told jokes and listened to them.

Once I worked for a farmer for several weeks, for nothing, because I just wanted to be around him to listen to him talk, to savor the sauce of his character, to collect his stories. His name was John Payne and he lived at Disputanta, Kentucky.

One of John's neighbors was a banjo-picking man named Tommy Dees. He told me this story about Tommy:

This city lawyer went to see Tommy about a matter and noticed a small fur lying in the corner, asked Tommy what it was. "I reckon it's a mink skin," Tommy said, in his droll, dry manner of speaking. "What'll you take for it?" the lawyer asked. "Oh, I reckon it ought to be worth about eight dollars."

The lawyer paid him, returned the next week, a little angry, to confront Tommy: "Tommy, you hoodwinked me! They told me down at the store that was a weasel skin . . . wasn't worth but two dollars!"

Tommy's face didn't change expression, but there might have been just the slightest twinkle in his eye

1

when he said, "Ahhh, you didn't let that feller beat you outa that mink, did you?"

I liked the twist in that bit of humor, and the understatement of it. But then, I like almost all kinds of humor. If it's funny, I laugh. I have heard humor explained and many people have put forth the theory that we laugh mostly because we feel superior, like seeing a guy slip on a banana peel. I don't agree with this *superior* theory. If the guy burns himself, I don't laugh. I sympathize with him.

And I think that's what I'm doing when I laugh at him, for whatever reason.

To me, comedy is an attitude. It has to do with how the joke is told. For instance, there's the one about the prisoners who were so familiar with the jokes that all they had to do was call out the number of the joke to get a laugh. Offering a demonstration to a visitor, the warden called out: "Number 97!" The prisoners howled in laughter. "Now you try one," said the warden.

The visitor yelled, "Number 3!" No laughter. "Number 13!" Still no laughter.

The warden said, "I guess it all depends on how you tell it."

The joke teller was not endowed with the comic spirit. His bearing, his attitude was not funny. Even when the joke is so funny it gets a laugh, in spite of the teller, the laugh is mirthless. It is a hollow laugh. *Some people have a weak sense of humor because they have a weak sense of people.*

Generally speaking, I don't like ethnic jokes. But I laugh in spite of myself, if they are funny. If they are not, I don't laugh. And it gives me a chance to zing something back at the would-be humorist, jumping on him for being prejudiced. (If I think he is.)

President Reagan uses humor effectively, while his former Secretary of the Interior, James Watt, could not buy a laugh and his attempts at humor finally cost him his job. It was not a matter of delivery. It was something in the attitude. And understanding. Reagan understood the delicacy of the comic spirit. He used humor as a tool to quiet his critics, to allay fears about his age, even to take the heat off James Watt.

For example, once in New York President Reagan delivered a great line at a ceremony involving the Westway highway project, apologizing to the crowd that James Watt would have been present, except that he was "on assignment strip-mining the Rose Garden."

President Reagan's humor adds to his charm and I think it helped him get re-elected in 1984.

As an entertainer (somewhat like Reagan but not as good-looking) I realized long ago the power and usefulness of humor. Sometimes people sit there and stare at you. In every audience there are a few sourpusses and it is hard to keep from looking at them. If you were nervous to begin with, glancing at their stony faces makes it worse.

So I tell a joke.

I get into a story, trying to relate to the audience, and if I am successful with my jokes, my singing goes better. I can see them relax. I can see them start to like me, because they know I like them. My jokes told them that.

A joke used this way is not a frail thing. It is a powerful thing. And the laughter it brings forth is from the audience's appreciation of being appreciated. Sometimes when I am on a roll I think I would like to have been a stand-up comedian or a humorist like Mark Twain. Then I realize that that would have been impossible for me, for I don't have the right face. I don't look funny. (By the way, you can't judge people by how they look, I realized long ago. Some of those sourpusses in the audience are the ones who come backstage after your show and tell you how much they liked it. Inside they are warm and wonderful people.)

Don Knotts sets you up to laugh just by walking on-stage. He looks funny. Flo, on the TV show *Alice,* is the same way. She plays that character so well, so sassy and brassy, you are prepared to laugh just by the attitude she creates. "Kiss my grits!" could be dirty, could even be menacing spoken by a villain, but when Flo says it it cracks you up.

My favorite country editor, Jim Comstock, has genius for creating and collecting humor. He has that attitude about him, that twinkle, that tells you before he speaks that it's going to be funny.

Editor of a "weakly" newspaper called the *West Virginia Hillbilly,* Jim has been "... drawn as by an irresistible magnet to good yarns and colorful characters and the ways, the wisdom, the passions and peccadillos of mountain folk," to quote Norman Corwin.

Here's a Jim Comstock story:

The old farmer was standing by the woman's car over on Leaping Branch, telling her how to get to Hell's Half-Acre, when this bird flew over and let him have it on the shoulder. They were both embarrassed, the city lady and the old farmer. And she was nice, because she asked him did he want a tissue. He said no, he reckoned not, because as fast as that damn bird was flying, it'd be to Charleston by now!

As many great stories, jokes, and character sketches as he has collected, Jim Comstock is himself the greatest story, the greatest character of all. Once when *Hillbilly* covered a ramp (wild onion) festival, Jim printed the issue with ink perfumed with ramps. (The Post Office scolded him for that!) He wrote an article about "How to Take Out Your Own Appendix," using a picture of the Venus de Milo statue to show where to make the incision marks, and it caused an international stir. Calls came in from London and all over from folks trying it, asking for further instructions! (Jim scolded himself for that one and quickly printed a follow-up, explaining that it was supposed to be all in fun, not taken seriously.)

Jim helps bear out the main point of my comments on humor. In spite of his barbed pen when he is irate, his caustic wit when he thinks someone is acting too pompous, behind all his jokes and editorials you know he loves the very ones he is giving the devil.

If he laughed seeing a man slip on a banana peel it would be because he saw himself in that man, and was laughing at himself.

My wife, Mary, reminded me today that there is one other important thing about comedy and humor. Jokes wouldn't be told if nobody laughed. The laughers, the appreciators, are as important as the jokers. Mary is a great laugher. Ordinary joke tellers soar to uncharted heights when Mary laughs. Sometimes I even think that maybe I did miss my calling, when I pull one off on her. Like, one day she asked me if I had seen the broom.

"Where did you leave it after your last flight?" I asked, and she roared.

She told me the garbage man complimented her on the way she looked one morning, "Ah-ha," I said, "so the ole garbage man is talking a little trash, huh?" She cracked up. Tears burst out of her eyes. Well, I know I'm not that great, but it feels good to get a laugh.

And, like Jim Comstock, I've been collecting stories, jokes, and funny songs (and making them up) all my life.

So has Loyal Jones. We put on a humor festival to see if we couldn't collect some more, with the idea of putting them all into a book. And this is it.

So here's to you, the reader, now the important ingredient called our audience. I hope you get some good laughs. I don't care if you laugh at us or with us or if you feel superior or inferior to us...I don't care why you laugh, or where, or how. Because no matter how you analyze it, when it's all said and done...it's either funny or it ain't.

Appalachian Humor

LOYAL JONES

A good laugh is better than a dose of salts.
—GRANNY MORGAN

Everything human is pathetic. The secret source of humor itself is not joy but sorrow.

—MARK TWAIN

Nowhere else in the country is the tragic view of the human condition so ingrained as in the South in general and the Appalachians in particular. Perhaps this is because we are closer to Calvinism than any other people. By Calvinism, I mean the system of theological thought that perceives human persons as flawed, unable to extract themselves from their own fleshly pursuits without the grace of God, that God alone decides who will be saved and who not and that there is nothing we can do about it, that the God who elects some of us to glory will keep us until the end, and that elected believers are equal. It is a grim system but it has its attributes. Calvinists are rarely surprised, almost never astonished, at our capacity to invent evil, and quite often they are pleasantly surprised that we are better than expected.

7

It is certainly true that the more optimistic gospel of the Methodists and others permeated the regions of the South, and many of us have tried to get the hang of perfectionism. We believe in God. We try to believe in goodness, in perfectability, but underneath is the fear that we are going it alone in the world and getting euchred—flawed, unreliable and absurd, pretending that we are worthy and in control. Yet we know that our dignity is a too-small hat in the winds of truth. All people know this, but here in this region we keep it uppermost in our minds so that the only reasonable thing to do about it is to laugh—at ourselves and at others who pretend, against odds, that all is well with the human enterprise.

It is easy to believe that such a view of life is passing from the American scene with the family farm, that urbanites would not be hounded by such. Yet recently, in a review in the *Saturday Review,* Mark Zussman wrote: "The world is more or less as it must be and the mature person approaches it with compassion, to be sure, but also with irony."

The mature person saves some compassion and most of the irony, or humor, for himself. This mature sense of things is a modest view. Such a person's humor is self-deprecating. It is also aimed at those who pretend to be what they are not, nor can be. Such a humor helps to create a proper perspective. It allows one to cope in a life that is often baffling and disappointing. It also comes from a defiant as well as humble heart. No one can evade disaster and death but we can escape the degradation of dreading and fearing the inevitable. That in itself is a victory.

Here in Appalachia we have seen our loved ones die in hazardous occupations and from unchecked diseases. We have been bilked of land, minerals, and ballads. We have been gerrymandered, lied to, and done unto. But we have endured, partially at least, because we could laugh.

There is also, of course, the lighthearted banter, the rusties (pranks) that are pulled on one another. In every community there is the wag, the prankster, who lightens the day with his antics. Some of this humor has a barb in it, ruffles dignity, but most of it is gentle wit, not aimed at embarrassment. It is surface humor, light and yet concerned with the distempers of the human spirit.

Some characteristics of southern mountaineers may be in order. Their absorption with religion has been alluded to. I have made a case for the inherent Calvinistic nature of the belief system. This is supported by the Appalachian writer and raconteur Harry Caudill, who claims that we are all Baptists. "Oh, you'll find Methodists, but if you scratch one you'll find a Baptist underneath." Indeed, the oldtime Baptist view of things does seem to explain Appalachians better than any other view. Many historians have given credit to Scotch-Irish Presbyterianism for shaping the character of those who settled the mountains, but Presbyterians tend to be middle-class and somewhat aloof from the common folks. Baptist theology attracts ordinary people, reinforces the leveling tendencies of mountaineers, and supports their basic radicalism. It seeps to the core, as Caudill suggests. I heard one fellow saying, "I used to be a Baptist." Another answered, "There is no such thing as an ex-Baptist!" There are probably more jokes about religion in the mountains than about any other subject. Why is this? In some parts of the country people are afraid to make jokes about religion because they might be perceived as sacrilegious. Here even the preachers tell jokes about their foibles and the inconsistencies of the church. Perhaps it is because they have not been overly imbued with the perfectionist zeal. They see and comment on follies, even religious ones. A well-known story is this:

A good Sister in the balcony of a church got happy and began to dance a little. She lost her balance and fell. However, her dress tail caught on a hanging light fixture, leaving her safely suspended but somewhat exposed. The preacher, thinking quickly, shouted, "The first man that looks upon this good Christian woman will be struck stone-blind."

There was a long pause and then came a hoarse whisper from a man down front: "I think I'll risk one eye."

Modesty, already mentioned, is rooted in the idea of not taking oneself too seriously. Mountaineers are levelers, believing that each is as good as another but no better. Such people are quick to note tendencies in themselves for pretending to be what they are not, and they make a joke about it. They are even quicker to note the tendency in others. Again the joke, or quip—as when my friend from West Jefferson, North Carolina, called.

"With whom did you wish to speak?" I inquired with English-teacher stiffness.

"You, you stuffy bastard," he responded.

Mountain politicians are hesitant to claim too much in the way of talent and ideals. They walk a thin line between modesty and affirmation of ability to do the job at hand. The rural voters love the official who can tell stories on himself, who doesn't get above his raising. The best story to illustrate these qualities was told by Fess Whitaker, of Letcher County, Kentucky, when he campaigned for jailer of the county:

You know, I was in Teddy Roosevelt's Rough Riders. I rode with him in the Battle of San Juan Hill in the Spanish-American War. I remember that day as if it was yesterday. Teddy and I rode stirrup to stirrup, our guns blazing and our sabers flashing in the sun, while off before us the Spaniards fled in a great cloud of dust. When we reached the top, Teddy reined up and said:

"We've done a great thing here today, Fess, and one of us is going to be President."

"You just go right ahead, Teddy," I said. "All I want is to be jailer of Letcher County."

Almost a contradiction of the value of modesty is the mountaineer's sense of independence and self-reliance,

reinforced by a stubborn pride. These traits are illustrated by the following anecdote, said to be true:

Several years ago there was a great snowfall in western North Carolina, and many people were snowed in for weeks. The Red Cross came to help. Two workers heard of an old lady way back in the mountains, living alone, and they set out to see about her, in a four-wheel-drive vehicle. They finally slipped and skidded over the mountain and got into the high cove where she lived, got out and knocked on her door.

When she appeared at the door, one of the workers said, "Hello, we're from the Red Cross," but before they could say anything else, she replied, "Well, I don't believe I'm going to be able to help you any. It's been a right hard winter."

Personalism is another trait of Appalachians. This means we think in terms of persons rather than degrees or professional reputations. We want to get you placed to see which Johnson you are. So we ask, "Whose boy are you?" "Are

you from the Horse Hollow Johnsons?" "Do I know your
Daddy?" "Are you the Johnson the tree fell on?" We tend
to get sidetracked from abstract discourses if we have a
good excuse to go off on a tangent and tell about some
interesting person who may or may not be closely related
to the discourse. Jeff Daniel Marion, the east Tennessee
poet, captures this tendency with a poem, "In a Southerly
Direction," a response to someone asking for directions:

> It's just
> over the knob
> there—
> you know the place,
> the one
> up there next to
> Beulah Justice,
> your mother's second cousin
> on her daddy's side.
> Or
> if you go in by
> the back road
> it's the farm across the way
> from Jesse's old barn
> that burned down
> last June
> with them 2 fine mules
> of his.
> Why hell, son,
> you can't miss it.

The late Joe Creason, who wrote a column for the *Louisville Courier-Journal,* used to tell a story about his visit
with a man in Pike County, Kentucky. They exchanged
howdys and commented on the weather, and then the man
asked, "Where are you from?" Creason told him he was
from Louisville. There was a long pause, and then the man
asked, "Who's the barber up there now?" The world of the
traditional Appalachian is a warm one of persons that one
knows or would like to know.

Appalachians have known more poverty and over a longer period than have most Americans. Therefore, hard-time jokes and allusions are a part of the fabric of life. The legendary invitations to hospitality were usually qualified with something like, "—if you don't mind staying with poor folks." My father told of being invited to dinner with a family who had only sorghum and cornbread but with the host graciously inviting them to "just reach and get anything you want." My father overdid it with the sorghum. The hostess, seeing his plight, offered to wash his plate for him. Expecting another dish, he complied, but when she returned the plate, nothing else was put on the table. When asked what he would "like to have now?" he replied, "I guess some more sorghum." William Sturgill, coal man and banker from Hazard, Kentucky, told the story about a woman going to see the governor about getting her husband out of the penitentiary.

"What is he in for?" the governor wanted to know.

"For stealing a ham."

"That doesn't sound too bad. Is he a good worker?"

"No, I wouldn't say that. He's pretty lazy."

"Oh. Well, he's good to you and the children, isn't he?"

"No, he's not. He's pretty mean to us, if you want to know the truth."

"Why would you want a man like that out of prison?"

"Well, Governor, we're out of ham."

One place name is Gnaw Bone, indicating that the people had to get every bit of nourishment they could from the food they had available.

The place names of the mountains contain a great deal of humor and irony. Consider: Hell-fer-Sartain, Beauty, Lovely, Sodom, Gizzard, Matrimony, Affinity, Bulltown, Only, 'Possum Kingdom, Pinchem Tight, Relief, Razor-blade, and Cheap. Place is very dear to mountain people. One fellow said he lived so far back in the hills that the sun set between his house and the main road.

Family is the functional unit of the mountains. It is extended, farflung, made up of individuals of diverse dispositions but held together by affection, obligation and

tradition. One wag, commenting on do-gooders, professors and the like who came to study mountaineers or do-unto them, commented, "The typical mountain family is made up of a father, mother, six children, four grandparents, a bunch of aunts, uncles, cousins, a sociologist, and a family planning specialist." One brother said to another, "You know, I've decided that Uncle Herman is a real S.O.B." The other considered this for a moment and replied. "Yeah, but he's our'n." Perhaps this attitude spawned the phrase "good old boy." One might say, "Jess is a good old boy," *even though* he drinks, beats his horse, or whatever. It is a tolerant acceptance of kin, warts and all. They are family. They can expect support when they need it.

My kinfolks represent generations of North Carolina mountaineers, a mixture of Welsh, Scotch-Irish, English, and Dutch (or German) stock, Baptist to the core. They did the best they could and then stood and took it. Grandpa Jones, a farmer and storekeeper, and Grandpa Morgan, a Baptist preacher-farmer, were both endowed with fiery Celtic tempers. Grandpa Jones was turned out of the church for fighting with his son-in-law over politics. It was said that they tore down a half-acre of corn, holding hands and kicking each other's tails in a merry-go-round of vituperation and retribution. Grandpa was an ardent Democrat, my uncle an ironclad Republican. Grandpa made terrible jokes about Hoover and the Republican Depression, asking my uncle if he knew that it was against the law to shoot up into the air before 9:00 a.m. When Uncle said he did not, Grandpa crowed, "Because you might hit somebody up in a persimmon tree getting his breakfast." This would nudge Uncle into a bitter and vindictive mood, because he was humorless when it came to politics. Grandpa Jones was a practical joker of the first water, always teasing children and leading adults into the bogs of his imagination.

Grandpa Morgan preached fiery sermons and was noted for the power of his rhetoric. He tolerated imperfections in members of his congregations until he could exhort them to mend their ways, but he had little patience with an errant horse or cow. He could blister the hair off the offending animal with his judgment on its intrinsic worth.

Humor around our house took the form of bantering, calling attention to inconsistencies and foibles. Practical jokes were in order. Gentle disparagement was used ironically, that is, really showing affection and approval even if the words indicated otherwise, as in: "You look like the hind wheels of hard time," or, "You must have been behind the door when the looks were passed out." Sometimes, though, the ridicule hurt, as when my brother's prize fighting cock got out of its cage and was slain by my mother's Rhode Island Red rooster. The threat of such ridicule kept us out of trouble at times. Once I was goaded into making a bid on a hip-shot, spavined, ancient and emaciated saddle horse, and I bid what I thought was a safe twenty dollars which was accepted with gleeful alacrity. I fled in dismay amid derisive comments, but this was better than the treatment I would have had if I had brought that decrepit horse home.

In church we devised games to play during the long sermons. One was to read off the hymn titles and add the words "under the covers." Thus we came up with such provocative and stimulating titles as: "Just as I Am Under the Covers," "Guide Me Under the Covers," and "A Wonderful Time Under the Covers." Of course we imagined that our parents would skin us alive if they found out about our sacrilege, not knowing that they probably had played the same game in their time.

It is a joy when your own children take up some of the same interests and tastes of their parents. Our children like and make mountain music. They love stories and humorous anecdotes. Yet I see a hesitation and sometimes a strained laugh when the old rural jokes are told. Their experience is different from ours. A generation is a long time in the twentieth century. Across the country a way of life, with references to agricultural terms, is passing. Just last month in the *Louisville Courier-Journal*, a journalist, obviously urban-spawned, reported that a federal judge, who grew up on the farm, was trying to decide "which was the easiest road to hoe" of two options in a legal case. My friend Jim Wayne Miller, who hails from Buncombe County, North Carolina, says that if the back-to-the-land movement keeps growing, we'll be having reverse malapropisms, such as "hitting the row" or "on the row again." All this reminds me of the stories I heard as a child of other children's misunderstanding the words to hymns—for example, one boy's fondness for the "cross-eyed bear hymn" ("Gladly the Cross I'd Bear") and the one about "Round John Virgin" ("'round yon Virgin"). A great deal of humor involves misunderstanding of words. As culture and experiences and interests, as well as localities, change, the possibilities for misunderstanding increase. It is both humorous and disquieting.

But life and culture and values go on, always changing. As Raymond K. McLain and Heraclitus say, culture and tradition are like a river, which appears the same but is ever-changing. No one of us can ever step into the same river twice. Yet we, like a river, always have the same basic characteristics. Our atoms change. Our children are different from us parents, but they are of the same genes and culture. Their tendencies and needs and desires will be similar to ours. Human nature is as it is, and we must be what we are, learn to live with it, and if we are to survive, we must laugh whenever we can.

Religion

There are three things that are real—God, human folly, and laughter. The first two are beyond our comprehension. So we must do what we can with the third.

—JOHN F. KENNEDY

A Conversation on Religion

A missionary came into the mountains to see how many people he could save for the Lord and from a way of life that he had read about in local color novels. He spied an old man sitting on his front porch enjoying the afternoon sun. He went up in the man's yard and without so much as a howdy said, "Brother, are you lost?"

"Why, no," the man said. "I've been living here forty years."

"I mean, have you found Jesus?"

"Now, I didn't realize he was lost. The Bible says he's in heaven until he comes again."

"What I mean is, are you a member of the Christian band?"

"No, but there is a Bill Christian who lives about five miles over the ridge."

19

"My question is, are you ready for the Judgment Day?"

"When is it?"

"It may be next week or it may be next year. We just don't know."

"Well, when you find out, you let me know. The old woman may want to go both days."

Loyal Jones

Going Prepared

A man was going down the road one day when he met an old friend, all dressed up from head to foot in hat, three-piece suit, fancy shirt and tie, and new shiny shoes, and with a Bible under his arm. He was surprised to see his friend dressed as he had never been seen before, and so he stopped to ask where he was going.

"Well, I'm going to Cincinnati. I've been hearing about the sporting houses up there, with all them good-looking women, and I aim to go up there and have me a time."

"But if you're going up to the sporting houses, why are you carrying your Bible?" his friend asked.

"If them sporting houses are as interesting as I hear tell," he answered, "I might just stay over till Sunday."

Dr. William Deal
Huntington, W.Va.

Peanuts

A new young preacher in a church was trying to call on all of the old people in the congregation who could no longer go to church. He went to a local nursing home to visit Aunt Sally, who was quite old. He was somewhat nervous, and he kept eating peanuts from a bowl beside her bed. When he got up to leave he suddenly became aware that he had eaten all of the peanuts.

"I'm so sorry. I ate up all of your peanuts," he stammered.

"Oh, that's all right," Aunt Sally said, "I'd already gummed all the chocolate off of them anyhow."

Shirley Jones
Marble, N.C.

Hillbilly Heaven

A man died and went to heaven. St. Peter met him at the front gate and took him on a tour. He saw the streets of gold, and listened to the heavenly choir accompanied by angels on harps. The newcomer agreed that heaven was a right nice place. Then he heard a wailing off in the far corner. He wandered over in that direction and presently saw a large group of people in chains, grumbling and dissatisfied.

"Who are those people?" he inquired of St. Peter.

"Those are hillbillies," said St. Peter.

"Why are they chained?"

"If we didn't do that, they'd go home every weekend."

Loyal Jones

The Priest and the Drunk

There was a Catholic priest who came out of a store one day and this drunk bumped into him and said, "My God, mister, you got your collar on backwards!"

He said, "No, you don't understand, I'm Father Jones."

He said, "Well, I got four kids myself, but I don't wear my collar turned around like that!"

The Catholic said, "No, you still don't understand. I'm the father of thousands."

The drunk said, "Well, buddy, you ought to turn your pants around backwards!"

Billy Edd Wheeler

The Graveyard Fence

Somebody in Virginia wrote to West Virginia master storyteller Riley Wilson, asking him to contribute to an old family graveyard fund for the purpose of building a fence around the graveyard.

Riley wrote back: "I don't think I care to contribute to a fence around a graveyard. You see, everybody that's outside doesn't want to get in, and those inside can't get out. So I don't reckon we need a fence."

Looking for Three Asses

Three smart-alecky boys met an old man, with long white hair and beard, out on the road. They decided to tease him.

"Hello, Father Abraham," said the first.

"Hello, Father Isaac," said the second.

"Hello, Father Jacob," said the third.

"I am neither Abraham, Isaac, nor Jacob," the old man responded. "I am Saul, son of Kish, and I am out looking for my father's asses, and lo, I have found them."*

Dr. Luther Ambrose
Berea, Ky.

Reluctant Sinner

A preacher was holding a revival, but he was having some difficulty in getting response from the congregation. One night he was striding back and forth on the raised platform behind the pulpit, exhorting his flock and urging sinners to approach the mourner's bench to repent their sins. Pacing back and forth with head uplifted, he stepped off the platform and fell flat on his face. When he remained motionless for a period of time, members of the congregation began to crane their necks to see their prostrate preacher. Finally, a man in the rear approached him and leaned over to shake him to see if he was all right. The preacher grabbed his hand, jumped up, and shouted, "One has come forward. Let us sing a hymn."

Jack Hall
Berea, Ky.

*I Samuel 9:3.

Kinfolks

The country preacher awoke one morning to find a dead mule on the highway in front of his home.

Calling the county health department in the county seat, he said, "This is Reverend Jones. There's a dead mule on the road in front of my house and I'd appreciate having it removed as promptly as possible."

The young clerk who answered the call thought he would have a little fun. "Uh, Reverend Jones," he said, "I always thought you preachers took care of the dead yourselves."

The preacher caught the kidding in the young man's tone, but he didn't let on. His reply was serious.

"We do. Yes. But in the case of jackasses we like to speak to the next of kin first."

Billy Edd Wheeler

Jordan Shrank

A Baptist preacher went to a Methodist baptizing. He sat and watched as the preacher sprinkled the converts from a small bowl. Since the baptizees were friends of his, after the service he rushed up to shake hands with them. However, as he went by the communion table, he hit it and sloshed the water out of the baptismal bowl. In a loud voice he proclaimed, "Uh-oh, I turned over Jordan."

Bonnie Dykeman
Asheville, N.C.

Christmas Crackers

For many years Appalachian people did not celebrate Christmas to any great extent, or else observed Old Christmas in January. However, when fireworks became available, many of the young people bought them and celebrated Christmas loudly and colorfully. One old mountain lady, observing a discharge of Roman candles and firecrackers, remarked, "You'd a thought that Jesus was a cavalry officer."

Loyal Jones

Getting Ready for the Preacher

A man was out plowing his corn when his son came and said, "The preacher wants to see you."

"Which preacher?" he asked.

"I don't know," his son answered.

"Well," the man said, "it'll take me about ten minutes to finish up here. You go back and find out which preacher it is. If it is the Methodist, lock up the chickens. If it is the Presbyterian, lock up the liquor. And if it's the Baptist, you get in your mother's lap and sit there until I come."

Thomas J. Dunigan
Berea, Ky.

What a Baptist Is, Is...

In Appalachia, somebody said, everybody is a Baptist, underneath it all. A Methodist is a Baptist who's afraid of water; a Presbyterian is a Baptist who went to college; an Episcopalian is a Baptist whose deals all worked out; a Unitarian is a Baptist who can't count; and a Catholic is a Baptist convert upon whom the full import of Calvinism has just dawned.

Loyal Jones

Blessed Are the Poor

The preacher began his statement with a modest disclaimer, "You know I am just a poor country preacher."

"I know," said an elderly woman. "I've heard you preach."

Rev. David Shill
Bluefield, W.Va.

No Fun

Question: What is the difference between a Methodist and a Baptist?

Answer: There isn't any difference. They both sin. It's just that the Methodist can't ever learn to enjoy it.

Loyal Jones

The Long Sermon

The pastor, waiting at the door, inquired of a lady parishioner, "Was my sermon too long?"

"No," she said, "it just seemed long."

"I'm sorry to hear that," said the pastor.

"Oh, don't be," said the lady. "It was one of the best long speeches I ever heard. I just thought it was superfluous."

"Good. I intend to have it published posthumously."

"I hope you hurry," the woman said. "I want to read it."

Wilma Dykeman
Newport, Tenn.

The Power of Prayer

There was this religious man who prayed long and loud at church and said that if you pray earnestly the Lord will protect you. One day this man went bear-hunting with another church member. He didn't take a gun, just went along for the trip. The dogs had a bear going, and it was mad. It came off the hill, saw this man and made for him. He didn't look worried, though. He just knelt and began to pray for the Lord to deliver him. He looked up and the bear was still coming. He prayed some more and looked up, and the bear was still coming. He jumped up and took off, outran the bear.

Afterwards, a fellow churchman asked him why he thought the Lord didn't stop the bear.

He said, "Well, prayer's good for a prayer meeting, but not for a bear meeting."

Ivan Amburgey
Pine Top, Ky.

The Testimony

One night after the sermon, the preacher called on the members of the congregation to testify about what the Good Lord had done for them. No one volunteered. He asked again, and still nobody spoke. Whereupon he called on old Uncle Henry, who was infirm and stooped with arthritis. "Tell us what the Lord has done for you, Uncle Henry."

The old man got up laboriously and slowly straightened himself.

"Well, He's might nigh ruint me," he said.

Wilma Dykeman
Newport, Tenn.

The Church Chandelier

A church was having its monthly business meeting. The treasury was in better shape than usual so the moderator asked if there were any special needs. One lady stood and said that she felt the church needed a chandelier.

A penny-pinching deacon jumped up and shouted, "I'm agin it and for three reasons. Number One, nobody would know how to spell it, Number Two, nobody would know how to play it, and Number Three, what this church needs is more light."

Loyal Jones

A Hole-ly Jesus

There was a preacher who would get ecstatic during his sermons and would look upward into the opening where the rope came down from the bell in the steeple and exclaim, "I see Jesus. I see Jesus!"

Some mischievous boys decided to play a trick on him, and so they constructed a figure that looked like a man, draped it with a sheet and stuck it up in the opening to the steeple.

That evening the preacher got inspired and started shouting, "I see Jesus." Then he looked up into the hole, saw the figure there, paused, and said somewhat hesitantly, "Hey, I *do* see something."

Loyal Jones

Converted Assets

A woman brought some bonds into the bank and presented them to the cashier.

"Are these for redemption or conversion?" he asked.

She came back with, "Is this the bank or the First Baptist Church?"

Loyal Jones

Charitable Contribution

An agent from the Internal Revenue Service called a preacher and said, "One of your church members, Sam Harris, put down on his income tax return that he had given $300 to the church. Is that true?"

The preacher thought a minute and replied, "If he didn't, he will."

Loyal Jones

Smoking Preacher

A Methodist preacher and a Disciple preacher were having dinner at the same house in Owsley County, Kentucky. When the Disciple finished his meal he filled and lit his pipe. The Methodist looked at him and said, "That's a sin, brother, and you ought to quit."

"No, I have scriptural authority for smoking," the Disciple replied.

"Where is it?" the Methodist asked.

"It's the verse right after the one that says you ought to sprinkle babies," the Disciple said.

Thomas Dunigan
Berea, Ky.
(As told by W.M. Mainous)

The Perfect Man

The preacher was preaching on the perfection of Jesus. He concluded that Jesus was the only perfect man. One member met him at the door and challenged this conclusion.

"I know one other perfect man," he said.

"Who was that?" asked the preacher.

"My wife's first husband," the man responded.

Loyal Jones

Noah's Wife

A preacher, ending his sermon, announced that he would preach on Noah and his Ark on the following Sunday. He gave the scriptural reference for the congregation to read ahead of time. A couple of mean boys noticed something interesting about the placement of the story of the Flood in the Bible. They slipped into the church and glued two pages of the pulpit Bible together. On the next Sunday the preacher got up to read his text.

"Noah took unto himself a wife," he began, "and she was . . ." He turned the page to continue, ". . . 300 cubits long, 50 wide and 30 high." He paused, scratched his head, turned the page back and read it silently, turned the page and continued reading.

Then he looked up at the congregation and said, "I've been reading this old Bible for nigh on to fifty years, but there are some things that are hard to believe."

Loyal Jones

Feeding the Cattle

The traveling preacher came to the small country church to preach the Sunday sermon, and only one man showed up. The preacher looked at his watch, finally walked down to the man, said, "Well, looks like we're not going to have a large congregation today. Maybe, since there's only one person here today, I won't preach at all. What do you say?"

The farmer looked at him, said, "Preacher, if I go down

to feed my cattle and just one shows up, I feed him. I don't turn him away hungry."

The preacher allowed as how the man was right, so he lit into a sermon wholeheartedly, and he preached for half an hour. Then he kept going, for an hour. The man looked at his watch but the preacher didn't slow down. He preached for an hour and forty minutes!

After the sermon he walked out to the man, said, "Well, what did you think of that?"

"Preacher," the man replied, "like I said, if I go down to feed my cows and only one cow shows up, I don't turn him away unfed. But then, I don't dump out the whole durn bucket, either."

Dr. Arthur M. Bannerman
Swannanoa, N.C.

Not the Regular Minister

While he was president of Warren Wilson College in the mountains of western North Carolina, Dr. Arthur M. Bannerman and his wife, Lucille, were invited to come and conduct a service in a small church out toward Madison County.

After the service, Mrs. Bannerman was approached by a lady who evidently didn't know who she was, for she said to Mrs. Bannerman, somewhat apologetically, "I hope you'll come back . . . he's not our regular minister!"

The returns on his sermon were mixed, Dr. Bannerman said, with his great good humor. One lady said, "That was right good, Mr. Bannerman. I'm glad that other feller couldn't come!"

While another lady told him, after he said he hoped he hadn't talked too long, "Oh, no, you didn't talk too long. It just *seemed* long!"

Billy Edd Wheeler

The Tight Rich Man

I like stories about people who are a little short on their contributions to the church. There was a man, back in the

Ozarks, who was rather wealthy but he wasn't giving anything to the church. They needed a new ceiling really bad and he was sitting in services one day when a piece of plaster came off and hit him on the head and brought some blood. So he stood up, rubbed his head and said gruffly, "I'll give ten dollars!"

A voice in the back of the church said, "Lord, hit him again!"

Dr. W. Gordon Ross
Berea, Ky.

A Damn Fine Sermon

Some friends of mine out in the Ozarks finally got a crusty old fellow to go to church. They wondered how in the world he would like it! He was very crusty and outspoken and they thought he was irreligious, but he really wasn't. Going out after the sermon, he said to the preacher, "Preacher, that was a damn fine sermon!"

And the preacher said, "Now, listen here, we don't talk that way around here!"

"Oh, I'm sorry . . . but I liked that sermon so much, I gave $25."

The preacher said, "The hell you did?"

Dr. W. Gordon Ross
Berea, Ky.

The Old Reprobate

One mountain area had a reprobate to die; he hadn't been good to his wife, had neglected his children, had never darkened the door of the church, was sober hardly a day in his life. He came to die, and they had a graveside service. In this particular community, the sage of the town was always called upon to say a few words about the people in the town that he had known all his life. People wondered what the sage would say about this old reprobate when nothing good, that they saw, could be said about him. But the sage came to make his statement about the deceased reprobate and he said, "Well now, beloved, you know he wasn't as bad *all* the time as he was *most* of the time!"

Dr. Lee Morris
Berea, Ky.

The Preacher Sees a Dog Fight

I've had a lot of preacher jokes and stories passed down to me down through the years and they're impossible to forget, dangerous to pass on; but I'll take a chance.

Seems that this mountain preacher was holding a revival. He was from the area. It was difficult to bring heaven to earth and deny the earth that you come from at the same time, but he was trying! He wanted the congregation's whole attention and was trying his best to get it when a dog fight broke out just outside the church house window. People were looking to see what was causing the ruckus and the mountain preacher could see better than anybody else, and he wanted to hold their attention, but he was watching the dog fight, too. He was into his preaching chant and he said something like this: "Now, take no heed to the dog fight, ah! You must be reverent in the church of God, ah! But bless my soul, ah! if that little dog ain't gonna whip the tar out of that big dog, ah!"

Dr. Lee Morris
Berea, Ky.

Guitars and Spittoons

Down home there were two deacons in our church who were sort of in competition. One of them had a guitar, and every Sunday he'd bring it and play and sing in church. The other deacon resented this, and one Sunday he said, "Why don't you get rid of that old guitar. You know, there ain't going to be no guitars in heaven."

"Oh, yes, there will be," the other one said. "I'm going to take this guitar with me and sing with the angels. We're going to have a joyful time. And while we're talking about heaven, why don't you get rid of that chew of tobacco in your jaw. There ain't going to be any tobacco in heaven, and there ain't going to be any spittoons. Where are you going to spit?"

"I'm going to spit right in the hole of your guitar."

Lewis Lamb
Paint Lick, Ky.

The Preacher and the Possum

There was an evangelist came in to the community from out West. He was traveling through the country holding revivals. He wanted to preach but they were building a new church. It wasn't finished. You could look up and see the rafters and beams, but he wanted to preach. He got warmed up and was going pretty good. Now this old possum had crawled up there on one of the beams, and he got disturbed and crawled out over the preacher and looked down at him—lay there just a-grinning.

The preacher looked up just as he said, "You gotta put your faith in . . . God-A'mighty, what a gopher!"

Glen Baker
Fairmont, W.Va.

Everybody Surprised

This guy knocked on the Pearly Gates, and he said, "I'd like to get in."

St. Peter said, "Did you die a violent or a natural death?"

The guy said, "Well, I lived on the 13th floor of the Calhoun Towers in Greenville, South Carolina. I traveled on the road quite a bit. I was a songwriter and an entertainer. I came home early from a trip one time, and I was standing there, trying to get my key in the lock. I thought I heard some rustling around in my apartment, and I finally got the door open, and there was my wife kinda red in the face, and I thought I smelled cigar smoke, and the curtain was blowing at the window. I went over to the window and looked out, and there's a guy down on the 12th floor balcony in his shorts, and I went into a rage of passion and grabbed up the refrigerator and pushed it out the window and it fell down and killed him. They found me guilty of murder and executed me and here I am."

St. Peter said, "Whew-o, step over to the side there. Next."

Another guy said, "I'd like to get in."

St. Peter said, "Did you die a violent or a natural death?"

The guy said, "Well, I live on the 12th floor of the Calhoun Towers in Greenville, South Carolina, and I stepped out on the balcony one hot night to get a breath of fresh air and I heard this noise, and I looked up and saw the bottom of a refrigerator and that's the last thing I remember."

St. Peter said, "Hmm, step over to the side there. Next."

Another guy said, "I'd like to get in."

St. Peter said, "Did you die a violent or a natural death?"

The guy said, "Well, I was in this refrigerator, see . . ."

> *Joe Bly*
> *Asheville, N.C.*

The Dog Ate the Sermon

The city preacher worked hard on his sermon most of the week, and re-typed it all up on Saturday night. But during the night his dog chewed it all up. He didn't notice until it was time to go to church. When he got in the pulpit, he said, "I had a nice sermon prepared for you this morning, but my dog chewed it up. I'm going to have to rely on the inspiration of the Lord today, but I promise to do better next Sunday."

> *Hon. Brooks Hays*
> *Little Rock, Ark.*
> *U.S. Representative 1942–58*

Damning with Saint Praise

The preacher had preached a vigorous and thoughtful sermon, and several of the congregation rushed up to congratulate him. One lady gushed, "Preacher, every sermon you preach is better than the next one."

Dr. Troy Eslinger
Jackson, Ky.

A Question About Virgin Birth

A young pastor took a rural church. Being recently out of the seminary with its heady theological discussions, he set up a series of lectures to deliver to his flock on Thursday evenings. His first topic was "Immaculate Conception," and he gave what he imagined to be an inspired and thorough lecture on the subject. When he had finished, he asked if there were questions, not really expecting any. A little old lady in the back raised her hand and inquired timidly, "Uh, what are its advantages?"

Loyal Jones

A Wonder to Behold

There was this rural church where one of the good brethren had as his self-ordained function keeping the air circulating through the church house, and about the middle of the service, he would get up and go over to the side and raise the window and let the air come through.

One Sunday morning this man got up to raise the window, as was his calling. He was a big, hefty man; had a big front; his belt was tight around his belly like a piece of baling wire around a sack of seed corn. He went over and jerked on the window and his belt came loose, and his pants fell down around his knees! And, of course, the reverence went out the window that he'd just raised.

And, ever since that event, every time he would go to the window, a hush would fall over the congregation as they waited for some great wonder to befall them again!

Dr. Lee Morris
Berea, Ky.

A Dream About Hell

I was brought up in a very strict religious home. In fact, when they had what we called protracted meetings, the preacher would bring all five or six of his kids—he'd usually have five or six—and he'd stay at our house for two weeks. They'd stay until the vittles ran out or the meeting closed, whichever came first.

One time I remember we were running low on wood, and my mother wanted to be polite, so she kept saying to me, "Stand back and let the preacher up to the fire." Well, I stood back until I froze. So, finally, I went to bed. And after I got warmed up real good I went to sleep and had a nightmare.

When morning came I came in through the kitchen and there's that preacher eating hotcakes like someone taking pills . . . you know, *gluck, gluck, gluck!* He said, "How are you this morning, young lady?" And I said, "I'm fine, but I had this horrible dream last night. I dreamed I was in this hot place and there was an old man with a pitchfork chasing me around."

He said, "Why, you know what that was? That was hell." (I said to myself, *it sure was!*) "Well, tell me, what was it like down there?"

I said, "Just like West Virginia. They just kept saying, 'Stand back and let the preacher up to the fire!'"

Bonnie Collins
West Union, W.Va.

Going to Heaven

A preacher was in the midst of a fiery revival, and he was at the height of oratory and exhortation. He described the terrors of hell and then with rapturous tones described heaven. Then he abruptly asked of the congregation:

"How many of you want to go to heaven?"

All of the faithful held up their hands except one old deacon, a veritable saint of the church. This surprised the preacher and he inquired, "Brother Davis, don't you want to go to heaven?"

"Yes, I do, Preacher, but you sound like you want to get up a bus-load tonight."

Loyal Jones

Preacher Talk

An old Baptist preacher was crossing the street when a teenager roared down the street in a hotrod, grazed the old preacher, and caused him to fall into the gutter.

The preacher jumped up, shook his fist and yelled, "You son-of-a-bitch. Have you no respect for a preacher?"

Loyal Jones

Hosea and the Devil

The most religious man in Iron Duff was Hosea (pronounced *Hosey*) Morrow. In addition to carrying the name of a prophet he carried himself through life with uprightness and a degree of moral perfection which spawned legends.

One Wednesday night on the way to church, Hosea met the Devil. He was just crossing the long footlog across the creek above the swimming hole when he saw him coming across from the other side . . . the old Devil himself.

"Go back, Hosea," said the Devil. "You don't need no more church anyhow!"

"You go back, Devil," replied Hosea. "You could use some!" And he walked straight on toward the old Devil.

The Devil could feel the actual vibrations of righteousness radiating off Hosea as he got close. He figured he better get out of good's way before all that concentrated holiness ruined him for life and eternity.

There wasn't time to tuck his old pointed tail and run, so the old Devil just took a belly-busting dive off the footlog into the swimming hole and, with the water just a-hissing, swam on out to the other side and disappeared into the wood.

Hosea wasn't even late for church.

Rev. Don Davis
High Point, N.C.

Preacher, You Missed My Mouth

One of the least religious men in Iron Duff was said to be Uncle Alf Jolly. A veteran of the Civil War, Uncle Alf told everybody in Iron Duff that he had been General Lee's right-hand man, and that General Lee had always called him "Uncle Alf" as a term of endearment and respect.

What the General was endeared to was a mystery, for Uncle Alf was in his later years as mean as they came. He was a voluminous drinker of corn likker, a volunteer fighter with about anybody, and one of the most blue-breathed cussers anybody had ever heard.

Uncle Alf rode a little blue mule and his long legs could almost wrap around its belly. He also had a long, full, white beard (usually full of cuckleburrs, beggar-lice and tobacco spit), which he could stuff inside his overalls when he worked, to keep it out of harm's way.

After living around him with full acceptance for many years, it was a great surprise to the people of Iron Duff when, after a long trip to Tennessee, Uncle Alf returned home to announce that he had "got religion," and was planning to change his ways.

"You all just wait till the spring of the year," he said. "When the water in the creek warms up, I'm a-going to get baptized, join the Baptist church, and be a Baptist."

Everybody did wait.

When springtime came there was a big revival at the Baptist church. Uncle Alf went and went forward. He made his profession and made plans (with several others) to be baptized the following Sunday afternoon.

Sunday afternoon came. It was a good warm day. The one thing everybody wondered about Uncle Alf was answered when he showed up. For the first time in memory his beard was all clean! It had been washed white as snow, and all brushed out until it covered his front like a baker's apron.

The preacher waded out into the water and prayed. Then he heisted, "Jesus, lover of my soul," and everybody joined in singing while he motioned to the candidates to start on out into the water. He got the first one under on "let me to thy bosom fly." Two more went down on "while the nearer waters roll, while the tempest still is nigh."

The only one left was Uncle Alf. As he had waded out into the water, his clean beard floated on top instead of sinking, and he was indeed a beautiful sight there in the water in the sunshine.

The preacher got him by the nose, and he went down. While Uncle Alf was being baptized all the people were singing:

> "Hide me, O my Savior, hide,
> Till the storm of life is past."

Then it was all over, except singing the last line:

> "Safe into the haven guide;
> O receive my soul at last!"

So, Uncle Alf was now a Baptist!

Things went quite well along through the summer. People were amazed at Uncle Alf's behavior—he really did seem to be quite different. (But gradually his beard did burr back up, get dirty as before, and become stained brown once again by tobacco juice.)

Perhaps the summer passed easily because there was no real encounter with temptation or idleness during the working season of the summer. However, when fall came, with it came Uncle Alf's first time of testing.

You see, the corn crop was by now all cut, put up, and in the process of being liquified. This year, for the first time in memory, Uncle Alf's presence and advice were not to be found near any of the stills in the north part of Haywood County.

Some of his old friends got to missing him, and one day decided that they needed his evaluation of the quality of their nightly produce.

So they filled up a couple of fruit jars of moonshine so

perfect that the beads would climb the sides of the jar if you didn't put a lid on.

With this small sample, they went over to Uncle Alf's to look for his evaluation.

"No sir!" he said. "I don't drink likker no more! Since I got religion I give up drinkin' likker. I promised the Baptists I wouldn't drink no more likker!"

It sounded like that was that, so Uncle Alf's friends (sadly) started to take their samples and leave.

"Wait a minute!" he said, just as they started out the door.

Uncle Alf went over to a shelf and opened a sack of brown sugar. He scooped up about half a cup of sugar and dumped it in one of the fruit jars of corn likker they had brought. Then he stirred the brown sugar around until it was swirling, and, before it had a chance to settle, Uncle Alf drank that brown sugar! "Whoooooo! I never promised the Baptists I wouldn't drink no sugar!" Uncle Alf hollered and clicked his heels together.

That event should have been a warning of things to come, but since everybody didn't know about it, nobody really paid that much attention. But gradually, as the weather got colder and colder as winter came on, Uncle Alf began drinking more and more sugar!

Then it happened. About Christmas time there was a big gathering of people for some kind of party and dance. Uncle Alf was there with his sack of sugar. There was also plenty of liquid corn to stir it up in. As the night went on the likker went down, the noise went up, and Uncle Alf's sugar gradually disappeared.

About that time a big fight broke out, and Uncle Alf happened to be right in the middle of it. He started biting, and people started scattering, but one feller from White Oak was too slow, and before he escaped, Uncle Alf bit a good-sized hunk out of the side of his ear!

By daylight the next day Uncle Alf was in jail.

His first visitor was the Baptist preacher, who wept until tears ran down his face when he talked to Uncle Alf. "Oh

me! Oh me!" he cried. "My heart's a-breaking! Here you
are . . . you were my finest example of a changed life . . .
(sob!) . . . and now you've gone and backslid worse than a
Methodist! Ooooh me!"

Uncle Alf looked the preacher straight in the eye. "It's
your fault!" he said.

Now this startled the old preacher. "What do you mean
it's my fault? Why, I baptized you!"

"That's why it's your fault," said Uncle Alf. "You told
me to get cleaned up to get baptized. I did—beard and
all."

"So what?" said the preacher.

"When my beard's clean, it floats!" said Alf. "When
you put me under, you didn't notice that that floating beard
kept you from seeing that you got every bit of me under the
water *but my mouth!*

"Yes, preacher, I'm 99 percent saved! . . . But you
missed my mouth. So it's your fault that I don't have no
control whatsoever over what my mouth says, eats, drinks,
or bites. Yessir, *you* done it!"

That's the way Uncle Alf told it, but some people say
that's not really the way it was. Yes, some people say that
the real truth is that the baptism was held in that same
swimming hole below the footlog where Hosea Morrow
had scared the Devil into swimming, and real fault was that
poor old Uncle Alf got baptized in Devil-water.

Since I heard the story both ways, I don't know who's
to blame for Uncle Alf's relapse: the preacher, the Devil,
or . . . maybe . . . neither one!

Rev. Don Davis
High Point, N.C.

Doctors and Lawyers

"A specialist is a man who learns more and more every day about less and less and finally knows everything about nothing. Whereas a general practitioner is a man who learns less and less every day about more and more until he knows nothing."

—SENATOR SAM ERVIN

Bedroom Physical

This elderly woman was sick, and had been for several weeks. Her children, who lived some distances away, came home one weekend to check on her. Since she was quite ill they called a young doctor who agreed to make a house call. When he came he asked the family to wait in the living room while he examined the woman in her bedroom. When he had finished, he came out, wrote a prescription, gave some instructions, and left. When the children went in to see their mother, she said brightly, "I really liked that young preacher."

The children looked at one another, and one said, "Why, Mother, that wasn't a preacher. That was the doctor."

The old lady reflected a moment and said, "Well, I guess he did get pretty familiar with me for a preacher."

Loyal Jones

Pain and More Pain

A man broke his arm and went to the doctor with it. The doctor examined it and got out a hypodermic syringe. The man said, "Doc, I don't need a painkiller. I've already had the worst pain there ever was, *twice.*"

So the doctor got the man on his table, put his foot in his armpit, tugged mightily until he got the arm set, put on a cast, and put the arm in a sling. Then he said, "I'm curious. What was the pain you talked about?"

"Well, the first time was when I sat down in a bear trap," the man said.

"What was the second?" the doctor persisted.

"That was when I run out of chain!"

Loyal Jones

Right Medicine, Wrong Disease

This man went to the doctor with a high fever. He gave him two or three kinds of medicine but it seemed to do him no good. When the man returned, the doctor studied the situation for a while and then said, "You know, I've never been much good on fever, but I've got some medicine that causes fits, and I'm hell on fits."

Loyal Jones

Mixed-Up Pills

That reminds me of Aunt Jenny Wilson of Peach Creek, West Virginia.

She asked me one time, "Billy Edd, did you hear about the lady that got her birth control pills mixed up with her saccharin tablets?"

And I said, "No . . ."

She said, "She had the *sweetest* little *baby.*"

Billy Edd Wheeler

No Stay-at-Home

A middle-aged woman went to see the doctor about hot flashes and other ill-defined symptoms. After examining her he asked, "Have you been through menopause?"

"No," she answered, "but I've been through Cudjo's Cave*."

Dr. Dan Robinette
Richmond, Ky.

Nice and Tan

A man in western North Carolina got sick and went to a doctor. The doctor treated him for a month or so and he seemed to get worse. Finally, the doctor told him that he thought he needed a change of climate and suggested that he go to Florida for the rest of the winter. So he moved to Florida, lay out in the sun, and got a good suntan, but in about two weeks he died. They shipped his body back to North Carolina.

At his funeral two of his old friends came by his casket to view him for the last time. He looked good with his suntan and new suit.

One friend said to the other, "Those two weeks in Florida sure did Sam a world of good."

Loyal Jones

A Lively Old Lady

A doctor made a house call on an elderly lady. She was sprightly and healthy, and he remarked on her good condition.

"Have you ever been bedridden?" he asked.

"Oh my, yes," she said. "Several times, and twice in a buggy."

Dr. Donald Hudson
Berea, Ky.

*A tourist attraction near Middlesborough, Ky.

One More Clean Shirt

A mountain woman in her nineties was approached by a man in his eighties complaining about his health. He enumerated his many complaints and illustrated them with examples of his suffering. The woman listened patiently and even sympathetically but finally she broke in and said, "It does look like about one more clean shirt will do you."

Ann Pollard
Berea, Ky.

A Cure for Three Ailments

A boy named Jack and some other fellows were courting the rich doctor's girl. The doctor said that anyone who could cure him of his three ailments could marry his daughter. His ailments were that he couldn't taste anything, couldn't tell the truth, and couldn't remember anything. Jack got some warm fresh rabbit pills, rolled them in sugar, took them to the doctor, and told him to take two of them. Asked, "What did them pills taste like, Doctor?"

"Tasted like rabbit manure rolled in sugar," the doctor answered.

"See, I've cured you of two of your ailments," Jack said.

"Yes," the doctor said, "but you haven't cured me of the third."

"Here, take two more of these pills," Jack said.

"Oh, no," shouted the doctor.

"See there," Jack said, "I cured you of all three."

Loyal Jones

The Doctor and the Dog

This country doctor got a call to go way back in the mountains to visit a man who was desperately ill. He drove as far as he could and then walked the last mile or so in the dark up a narrow trail. At last he saw the house. When he went up on the porch, a huge hound ran up and started jumping on him, whining and barking, so that it was hard for the doctor to get to the front door and knock. When the lady of the house opened the door, the dog bounded into the room and jumped upon the bed where the sick man lay. The doctor tried to examine the man, but the dog was astride him licking him in the face. The doctor kept looking at the woman, hoping she would do something about the dog, but she made no offer to help. So he proceeded, holding the dog off as best he could, not wanting to get rough with it because he knew how touchy some mountain people are about their dogs.

Finally he finished his examination, gave the woman some pills for her husband, took his payment, and said goodbye. He went out, closing the door behind him, but before he got down the porch steps, the woman opened the door and yelled, "Hey, Doctor, you forgot your dog."

Loyal Jones

The Ear

I want to tell you about two young fellows who got into a disagreement.

They had a real big fight and both of them survived it, but one of them who had lost an ear decided to take the other one to court. So he went and got him indicted. When the trial came up, the defendant hired a real polished lawyer to handle his defense.

When he cross-examined the first witness—a young fellow, a real mountaineer who hadn't bothered to go to school, but who wasn't a dummy either—the lawyer asked, "Did you see the altercation?"

"No, but I saw a damn good fight."

So the lawyer said several other things, asked questions, pushed beyond the normal amount of questioning. Then he came to the question of the plaintiff's ear being bit off in the fight.

"Don't you think it was possible that he got his ear caught in a sycamore root and tore it off?"

"Well, I thought that might have happened too," the witness said, "until I saw the other feller spit his ear out."

Roy Turner
Berea, Ky.

Witness

A witness was called to the stand to testify about a head-on automobile collision he had observed from his front porch. "Whose fault was this wreck?" the lawyer asked.

"Well, the best I could see," he said, "they hit each other at about the same time."

Loyal Jones

Independence

An old man went to town to buy some things. As he was crossing the street, a car came around the corner and hit him. He went up in the air, landed on the hood of the car, bounced off and hit the street. The driver jumped out of the car, helped the man up, apologized and offered to take him to the hospital. The old man felt himself over, stretched his neck tentatively and said, "No, no, I feel fine." The driver insisted on taking him to a doctor, but he declined. So the man got into his car and drove away.

A lawyer, a kinsman of the man who had been hit, had watched the entire affair. After noting down the license number of the car, he came over and said, "I saw what happened. Let's sue him."

The old man said, "No, I wouldn't want to do that. I'm all right."

The lawyer persisted, "Listen, I know how bad your arthritis is. I know this must have made it worse."

The old man craned his neck, turned his head back and

forth a few times and said, "No, you know I believe it holped* me."

Buck Henson
Wise, Va.

---

*"Holp" is an old-fashioned form of "help."

Schools and Book Learning

Keeping a collection of humorous items was not beneath the dignity of the great inventor Thomas Alva Edison. After he died, his son discovered a drawer of his desk stuffed with scraps of paper and clippings bearing jokes and quips. One of the witticisms therein said: "When down in the mouth, remember Jonah. He came out all right."

Napoleon in the Rockies

Down at Pine Mountain, in Harlan County, Kentucky, lived an old fiddler called Fiddling John Lewis. A college professor who was interested in folk music heard about him and went to see if he could collect some tunes from him. Mr. Lewis was hospitable and agreed to take out his fiddle and play for the professor. He played several tunes and played them well, and the professor complimented him on both his playing and the quality of his tunes.

"Those are nice tunes," he said. "Why don't you play me your favorite tune?"

So Fiddling John really put his heart and soul into a tune the professor had never heard. He was impressed.

"That was a beautiful tune," he said, "and you played it well. What do you call it?"

"That one is called 'Napoleon Crossing the Rockies,'" the old man said.

The professor was a professor, and he felt that he had to confront falsehood wherever he found it and to establish truth.

"That is a good tune, and you play it beautifully," he said, "but, you know, Napoleon never crossed the Rockies."

The old man reflected and then said, "Well, historians differ."

Dr. Francis S. Hutchins
Berea, Ky.

Historical Observation

A teacher assigned each of his students to make a speech on some aspect of American history. One boy chose George Washington as his subject. On the day of his speech he was very nervous. He went to the front of the room, flushed and gulped and finally came out with, "George Washington is dead, and I don't feel too good myself."

Loyal Jones

Appalachian Studies

With all the talk about ethnic studies and black English and Appalachian speech, I thought it was time to create a course in Appalachian math. In it students would study the following concepts: several, a few, a couple, a right smart, a mess, a little piece, a whole heap, a tad bit and a smidgin.

Loyal Jones

Education

A young boy in a country school brought in the wastebasket from the hall and said to the teacher, "I fotched the wastebasket." When the teacher looked at him disapprovingly, he said obligingly, "Looky there! I said fotched when I knew to say brung."

Byron Crawford
Bagdad, Ky.

No School Today
An education-conscious man encountered a young boy on a weekday during normal school hours.

"Aren't you having school today?" he asked.

"Nope," was the reply.

"Why not?"

"We busted the basketball."

Hilda Woodie
Berea, Ky.

Learning by Doing
The teacher was trying to teach gender in her grammar class. "What gender is cat?" she asked.

A little boy raised his hand in the back of the room. "Bring me the cat, and I'll see," he said.

Loyal Jones

Speaking Algebra
This farmer in Boone County, West Virginia, sent his son off to college. The boy decided to major in math. As soon as the boy came home after graduation the farmer couldn't wait to take him down to the country store and show him off.

The boy was a little embarrassed by it all, but he loved his dad and was grateful to him for helping finance his education. So he went along with it. As soon as they got to the store, the farmer proudly exclaimed, "Here's my son, fellers, home from college with a degree in algebra!"

He turned to his son and said, "Well, don't be bashful, boy, say something to them in algebra."

The son blushed and said, "Okay . . . pi-r-square."

The farmer got very flustered at that, blushed himself, and said, "Don't be silly, boy! Pie are round. *Cornbread* are square!"

Billy Edd Wheeler

The Cow

This little fellow, he's in kindergarten, and today is the day he's supposed to stand up on the stage and recite. He's supposed to describe a cow.

Now, he's not scared. Why should he be scared? His teacher is standing there watching in the wings, and out front there's just a few people . . . his parents and the parents of his friends . . . not a great *big* audience. Naw, he's not scared. He's *terrified!* The poor little guy stands there crossing his arms and touching his knees, twisting and squirming, and finally he begins:

"The cow . . ." (Long pause.) "Uh, the cow has . . .". (Long pause, a turn to look at the teacher, who urges him on.) "The cow has four legs . . . two horns . . . uh, four of these . . . you know, four . . ." He has now tied himself into a pretzel, paused again, looked for help to the teacher in the wings. Finally, in one quick burst, he makes another stab at it, this time in his own language. He says, "The cow ... the cow has four stand-uppers, four hanger-downers, two hookers and a swisher!"

Joe Bly
Asheville, N.C.

Investigator

Back at the turn of the century, at Berea College, President William G. Frost got wind of the trick that the girls in Ladies Hall were using to get boys in the dorm at night for a little coffee or a visit. The boy would come and toss a pebble up to the window, whereupon several girls would lower a large bucket down with a rope, the guy would step in it, and they'd pull him up.

President Frost heard about this and thought he'd investigate. So he went out one night—all on his own—tossed up a pebble, and sure enough, here came the bucket and he got in it. When the girls got him up to the windowsill, they realized who it was, dropped him, and broke his arm!

Billy Edd Wheeler

The Declaration of Independence

This Kentucky teacher was quizzing her students. "Johnny, who signed the Declaration of Independence?" He was older than some of the others. He said, "Damned if I know." She was a little put out by his swearing, so she told him to go home and to bring his father with him when he came back.

Next day the father came with his son, sat in the back of the room to observe, as the teacher requested. She started back in on her quiz and finally got back to the boy. "Now, Johnny, I'll ask you again. Who signed the Declaration of Independence?"

"Well, hell, teacher," Johnny said, "I told you I didn't know."

The father jumped up in the back, pointed a stern finger at his son, and said, "Johnny, if you signed that thing, you own up to it!"

Dr. Eslie Asbury
Carlisle, Ky.

Politics

Israeli psychiatrist Arnold Mishkinsky calls humor the "courage mechanism." Through humor, he says, man accepts himself as a mortal creature, prone to failure and living in fear, yet always capable of coping anew.

Yet the favorite move of most Americans faced with a challenge is to work harder. They don't realize that if they would season their labor with a touch of humorous insight and a dash of wit their challenges would be more easily overcome.

He who laughs . . . lasts.

—STEPHEN A. FRANZMEIER

Politician and Mountaineer

A state legislator was running for re-election, going about shaking hands and asking for votes. When he asked one old mountain man for his vote, the man replied, "I got me a theory about politicians."

"What's that?" the legislator asked.

"Well, if you elect a politician to one term, he learns to do his job. If you elect him to a second term, he learns to steal."

"Now, I don't look like I would steal, do I?" the politician asked.

"No, but you look like a slow learner," the old man said.

Bill Weinberg
Hindman, Ky.

Silent Elephant at a Donkey Parade

A woman from a staunch Republican family in east Tennessee was in court accusing a man of making improper advances toward her during a parade for a Democratic candidate for governor.

"Why didn't you cry out for help, if he was bothering you as you allege?" the man's defense lawyer asked her.

"You'll never hear me a-hollerin' at a Democratic parade," she answered.

Loyal Jones

The Long and the Short of It

A local politician had begun his speech from the steps of the courthouse. A heckler interrupted by yelling, "Take a minute and tell us everything you know."

"I'll tell all both of us know," the speaker retorted. "And it won't take any longer."

Loyal Jones

Kentucky Politics

Insinuations about corruption in Kentucky politics have often appeared in the reports of East Coast writers. A New York reporter came here to cover an election and dwelled on the low salaries paid to state office-holders—said they had to steal to make a living.

For example, the writer said, a young man went to a veteran Kentucky legislator to get his consent to marry his daughter. The boy said, "Sir, I must confess . . . my father spent two years in jail for horse stealing."

The veteran replied, "Well, son, that's nothing. I've spent four years in the Kentucky legislature."

Dr. Eslie Asbury
Carlisle, Ky.

The Assassination of Adolph Hitler

One of the funniest stories I ever heard came out of the Kentucky hills.

One winter day in the early forties a bunch of mountaineers were sitting around a pot-bellied stove at a country store listening to the news of the war when one of them asked, "Why doesn't somebody just shoot Hitler?"

"Well, they would," said another, "but nobody can get to him. He's too protected and everywhere he goes there's somebody there with him."

"I could get to him," said the first speaker confidently.

"How would *you* get to Hitler?" his friends asked.

"I could get to him all right."

"Well, just how would you do it? Tell us all and we'll call Roosevelt and tell him."

"All right," he said, "here's what I'd do. Some morning 'fore sunrise I'd get my rifle-gun and go up on the hill overlooking his house. I'd just wait there till he come out on the back porch to take his morning leak and then I'd pick him off."

Dr. Robert J. Higgs
Johnson City, Tenn.

World War II

A group of loafers around an Appalachian country store heard the news of the invasion of Normandy. They sat in silence for a few minutes, and then one man looked up at the sky, which was clear and blue, and remarked, "They shore picked a good day for it."

A mountain woman, hearing of the Germans' march into the Low Countries, said, "I wish Hitler would get married and settle down."

Loyal Jones

Hitler's Last Days

Dr. Benjamin J. Bush, once the pastor of the Warren Wilson College Presbyterian Church, came back to speak at the college after the War. He had worked for some time for the World Council of Churches in Geneva and told about the destruction in Berlin.

Everything had been leveled. As Dr. Bush talked about the last days of Hitler, he described the very spot where Hitler met his death, burned up in the bunkers, along with his paramour. Later when he was having lunch, family style, in the college dining hall, he discovered that something about his speech troubled one of the mountain boys.

"I can understand," the boy said, "why they'd burn up Hitler. But why'd they have to burn up a good *power mower* like that?"

Billy Edd Wheeler

Farming

An onion can make people cry, but there has never been a
vegetable invented to make them laugh.

—ANONYMOUS

Unsanitary Pork

There's a man in Doddridge County where I live. Well,
he's kind of a character. He lives right in my neighbor-
hood, and I hope they never make him clean up his yard,
because it makes my house look good.

He lives up on the hillside and his front porch is high off
the ground. He was raising hogs under there. So the
County Sanitarian came out and said, "Well, Mr. So-and-
so..." (wouldn't dare tell you his name, 'cause this is
true)...he said, "Mr. So-and-so, you can't raise hogs
under your porch."

"Why not?"

He said, "Well, it's not sanitary."

"What do you mean, not sanitary?"

He said, "Well, it isn't healthy."

The man replied, "Well, hell, I ain't lost a hog yet!"

Bonnie Collins
West Union, W.Va.

61

Three-Legged Chicken

A fellow was driving through the mountains of Kentucky when he looked over beside the car and there was a chicken running along at the same speed. He sped up, and the chicken did too, stayed right there beside the car. Then he noticed that the chicken had three legs, all three of them going so fast he couldn't be sure he had seen what he thought he had. He sped up to about eighty, and the chicken stayed right with him. However, when they got to a house beside the road, the chicken veered off and disappeared into the woods. The driver slammed on his brakes and backed up to the house. A man was sitting on the porch.

"Am I seeing right?" the driver asked. "Did that chicken have three legs?"

"Yep," the man said. "The woods back there are full of them. We're raising them for Kentucky Fried Chicken."

"I'll bet you're making a fortune, aren't you?"

"Not a cent. Ain't caught one yet!"

Dr. Charles Harris
Berea, Ky.

Growing Hogs

A farmer grew a lot of hogs on his hillside. He mostly let them roam in the woods, eat acorns, and root for whatever they could find. Occasionally he would feed them some shelled corn. The county agent came by to give him some advice, which was that he ought to use commercial hog feed. His main argument was that, on a balanced diet, the hogs would grow off and fatten faster. "That way you save a lot of time," he argued.

The farmer reflected and said, "What's time to a hog?"

Dr. Francis S. Hutchins
Berea, Ky.

Farmers

There were these three tenant farmers and it had been a very dry year. And, of course, they'd gone in hock for their seeds, fertilizer, and everything else that goes along with raising a crop of cotton. When they got to the gin, not one of them had enough for a bale! So they decided to combine their cotton to make one big bale; they were very down and out, but somewhere they come up with a jug of white lightning! And things begin to perk up!

Finally, one of the men jumped up and said, "When I sell my cotton, I'm going to buy my wife a brand-new sewing machine. She's always wanted a sewing machine and I'm glad now I can buy it for her."

The next man said, "Well, my wife has always wanted a washing machine; one of those kinds that runs on itself; and, when I sell my cotton, I'm going to get her a washing machine!"

The third man hadn't said a word.

Finally the men said to him, "Zeke, what are you going to do for your wife?"

He says, "Pass me that jug again; I ain't out of debt yet!"

> *Moir Pilson*
> *Stuart, Va., and Long Beach, Cal.*

A Pig Tale

One day I went to see a friend on his farm. He showed me about the place. We came to the pigpen. There was the strangest-looking pig I had ever seen. It had a *wooden peg-leg!*

We went to the house and my curiosity got the best of me; I asked about the unusual pig.

"One night *that* pig woke us up, busting down the door, squealing. The house was on fire. He saved our lives.

"Another time," he continued, "my tractor overturned, pinning me to the ground. Nobody around—thought I was a goner. Well, here came *that* pig running. He grunted and pushed till he got that tractor off me."

"Amazing," I exclaimed. "But why the wooden leg?"

"Hell, man! You don't eat a great pig like that all at one time!"

Bill Reed
Lexington, Ky.

Of Hogs and Men

Two brothers were arguing over the best way to raise hogs. One bragged, "I know hogs. I grew up with hogs."

The second one retorted, "Yeah, and you never got above your raising."

Loyal Jones

Me a Pint, Jay a Pint, and Bal a Pint

A poor widow lived on our creek with her two small grandsons, Jay and Bal. She tried her best to make ends meet from one year to the next by growing a good garden, a few small truck patches, and an acre or two of corn for her bread, preparing the soil and cultivating with her hoe. In late winter her cow died.

Hearing that Big Nelse Boggs, a prosperous farmer and storekeeper, had a cow to sell, she trudged with a basket of eggs for barter on her arm to his store one cold day, her head wrapped with a dark "fascinator" under her deep black poke bonnet. After she had traded, she stood for a moment at the counter, before asking in her deep, slow voice, "Mr. Boggs, have you got ary milk cow you would sell?"

"Yes, I have a young cow that came fresh last spring that I would like to sell."

"How much air ye a-astin' for 'er?"

"Thirty-five dollars."

"How much milk does she give?"

"Oh, I don't know for sure. About a gallon, I reckon."

The old lady was thoughtful for a few moments. "Well,

I don't want her, I guess. I don't want a cow that gives that much milk. I want a cow that will give me a pint, Jay a pint, and Bal a pint."

Dr. Cratis D. Williams
Boone, N.C.

Alcohol

I can't say whether we had more wit amongst us than usual, but I am certain we had more laughing, which answered the end as well.

—OLIVER GOLDSMITH

Trapped

One time this drunk was going across the graveyard when he fell into a freshly dug grave. It had been raining, so the mud on the sides of the grave was slick. He kept slipping back when he tried to climb out. He yelled for a while and nobody heard him, so he finally got tired and just sat over in the corner, and went to sleep.

Another drunk came along during the night and fell in there with him. He, too, started trying to climb out, without much luck. Until the first drunk woke up. He watched the guy jumping, clawing at the mud, trying to get out of there, until the guy got tired and stood there in silence for a second.

He spoke from his dark corner, "Might as well relax, buddy, you'll never get out of this place."

But he did!

Billy Edd Wheeler

The Long Stairs

I heard a story about a train track one time. These two old drunks were just barely able to stand, but they were going to try and get on a train. They went downstairs and somehow got on the track, thinking they were still on the stairs. They must have walked a half-mile when one of them said, "Boy, I've never seen such a long, long set of stairs!"

The other drunk said, "These low banisters are pretty rough, too, ain't they?"

Billy Edd Wheeler

Don't Tell It All

A man from western North Carolina was bad to drink. Once when he had been out on a drunk for several days, he came home sick and weak and asked his wife to pray for him.

She started out, "O Lord, please help this old drunken fool."

The man raised his head and whispered weakly, "Don't tell Him I'm drunk. Just tell Him I'm sick."

Hon. Felix Alley
Cashiers, N.C.

Milk and Beer

Two fellows went into a restaurant. One had recently got religion and, when the waitress asked him what he wanted to drink, he said he wanted milk.

The other man said, "Bring him a beer. He likes beer."

The waitress went away, and the first man said, "The Lord heard me order milk."

Loyal Jones

Only Two Beers

We had a judge in Haywood County who spent the whole morning trying drunk drivers. One after another they came before him and swore they'd only had two beers, and just happened to blow an 18 on the breathalyzer.

The judge ran out of patience. He said, "The next man that steps before this Bar of Justice and tells me he blew a 20 on the breathalyzer and then tells me he only had two beers . . . is going to spend the next six months in jail!"

Next case. This young man steps up and the judge says, "Son, what are you charged with?"

He answers, "I was charged with driving drunk."

The judge asked him, "What did you blow on the breathalyzer?"

The boy said, "I don't rightly remember, Your Honor, but I think it was about 22."

"That's a pretty good score," the judge said. "How much did you have to drink?"

"Your Honor," the boy said earnestly, "I don't remember exactly. It was either one or three. But it sure as hell wasn't *two!*"

Bob Terrell
Asheville, N.C.

Brr, It's Cold Down Here!

A drunk stumbled out of the local tavern and decided he'd take the short cut home, so he cut across the cemetery. It was dark, so he stumbled into a freshly dug grave. Couldn't get out. So he started yelling at the top of his lungs.

Finally another drunk from the tavern heard him, walked cautiously to the edge of the grave and looked down. "What's the matter?" he said.

The first drunk said, "Lordy, mister, you got to help me. I'm about to freeze to death down here!"

"Why, no wonder!" the second drunk said. "You ain't got no dirt on you."

Billy Edd Wheeler

A Clear Unknown Substance

I'm from Tucker's Knob, Tennessee, and I'll tell you folks, I like to never got here. I thought I'd take a short cut and run over here through Harlan County, Kentucky, but I got lost . . . the road turned into a gravel road, then a dirt road and then a little ole road that run up a tree. I finally turned around and started out of there when a great big old mountain man about seven feet tall jumped out of the laurels, into the middle of the road, and commenced waving his hands.

He climbed into my pickup and we drove about four miles, didn't say a word. Finally he pulled a Mason jar out of his sheepskin coat that had some clear, unknown substance in it, shoved it over to me, said, "Here, boy, have a drink!" I said, no, thank you, and he looked at me with those little ole beady eyes, said, "Boy, have a drink!"

I said, "No, now, I ain't drinking none of that moonshine!"

He pulled out a gun about that long, had a barrel big around as a hoe handle, stuck it in my ribs, said, "Boy, when I say have a drink, I mean, have a drink!"

Well. I submitted to temptation on the spot. That liquid fire burnt clean to my shoe soles, my heart quit beating and I went blind for about five minutes. When I could breathe again, I said, "Whew! How in the world can you stand to drink that stuff?"

He handed me the gun. He said, "I can't hardly. Here's the gun. Now you hold it on me and make me take a drink, will you?"

Ernest "Doc" McConnell
Rogersville, Tenn.

Joshua's Moon

An old man named Joshua was indicted for making moonshine and was brought to trial. The judge, who fancied himself a humorist, inquired of him, "Are you the Joshua who made the sun stand still?"

"No, Your Honor," the old man replied, "I'm the Joshua who made the moonshine still."

Byard Ray
Marshall, N.C.

He Died Happy

A group of people was sitting around at the wake of a man who had died the unusual death of drowning in a barrel of whiskey mash at the still he was operating.

His wife was wringing her hands and carrying on in a pitiful way.

"I wouldn't take it too hard, ma'am," her husband's fellow moonshiner said. "I think he died happy. He got out and went to the bathroom three times before he died."

Glen Baker
Fairmont, W.Va.

Longevity

Old Man, Young Woman

There's an old fellow in my community—I live in Fairview, North Carolina—I guess everybody has a Fairview where they live and they think it's just a suburb somewhere beyond a shopping center; but that's not what it is where I live. Fairview is called that because that's what we've got . . . you see, up on the mountain—we live in the mountains and up on top of the mountain, there is a community called "Great View" and then we live down a little lower on the mountain and it's called a "Fair View"; and, on down at the bottom, there's a little community called "Cain't See Nuttin'."

We have an old fellow there named Old Leo, and Old Leo is a good friend of mine. His first wife died when he was eighty-six years old, and when he was ninety he fell in love with an eighteen-year-old girl. Well, that got me kinda worried, because I didn't want to lose him 'cause Leo's a good banjo player, and so I went to talk to him.

I said, "Leo, I'm concerned. 'Cause there's things a person does when they get married and git their heart all excited and git their heart all stimulated and, well, it has been known to kill people before."

Leo thought about that awhile and he said, "Well, David, I figure, if she dies, she dies."

Well, they lived together for about six months. And he was starting to feel pretty bad, so he went to the doctor and the doctor said, "Now, Leo, you're just going to have to cut out having so much fun. If you don't, it could be the end of you!"

So Leo went home and told his wife that, feeling terrible, and said, "I'll take the upstairs bedroom, and you stay in the downstairs room." So they lived like that for about three months. And in the middle of the night one night, Old Leo started downstairs, but he happened to meet his wife on the stairs on the way up!

She said, "What are you doing coming down the stairs?"

He said, "I'm coming down to die! But what are you doing coming up?"

She said, "I'm coming up to kill ya!"

David Holt
Fairview, N.C.

Watch That Tree

There's this feller over in Pulaski County, his wife died. Had the undertaker come for her. They carried the body out the front door on a big board, across the porch, down the steps. And as they went across the yard, headed for the hearse, that board bumped against a maple tree there in the yard. And the woman stirred. And they begun to work with her, and she revived up.

That woman lived another ten years! Then she died again. And when the undertakers come for her this time and started across the yard with her, her husband said, "Uh, boys, watch out for that tree there."

Dr. Jim Wayne Miller
Bowling Green, Ky.

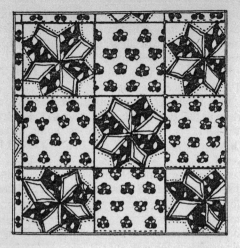

False Teeth

A friend of mine name of Captain Midnight (Roger Scutt was his real name) walked up to me one day and proudly flashed a pearly white smile at me. Pointing at his shining row of perfect teeth, he said, "How do you like 'em?" Before I could answer, he said, "Got 'em free today ... down at the morgue. They took 'em off this guy and gave 'em to me. Said they only had three meals on 'em!" (He smiled that twinkly, crooked smile of his that seemed to say, "Hey, you think I'm kidding, don't you, but maybe I ain't! Then again, maybe I am.") Captain Midnight used to run around a lot with Waylon Jennings. I had breakfast one time with him and Waylon's wife, Jessi Colter. This was about three months after his false teeth story. But then I guess they had about 270 more meals on them, if he was eating regular, which I doubt he was, because he hung out with his friend, Jack Daniels. Captain didn't like to drink on a full stomach!

Speaking of false teeth, there were two guys living at this boardinghouse that never would sit down at the same table together. One would eat and go upstairs, the other one would come down and eat. Everybody just knew there

was bad blood between those two guys.

Wasn't any such thing. They only had one set of teeth between them! After one ate, he'd go upstairs, take out his teeth, rinse them off and give them to the other guy. Then he'd come down and eat!

Billy Edd Wheeler

More False Teeth

Well, there was a convention going on, and the main speaker was sitting back in a chair and he happened to think he'd forgotten his dentures—they were back in the motel! He nudged the fellow beside him and said, "I've got to go back to the motel and get my dentures!"

The man said, "Wait a minute." He reached down in one pocket and pulled out a pair and said, "Here, try these."

The speaker tried them and said, "No, they won't work!"

The other man said, "Well, wait a minute!" So, down in another pocket he went and got another set and handed them to him.

He tried them and said, "Hey, that's pretty good. I believe I can use them!" After it was all over, he said, "Say, I was pretty lucky to be seated next to a dentist!"

The man said, "Dentist! I'm an undertaker!"

Glen Baker
Fairmont, W.Va.

Conversation

Two octogenarians sat on a bench by the courthouse. One of them said to the other, "Sure is windy today, ain't it?"

"Wednesday?" his friend said. "I thought it was Thursday."

"Thirsty?" his friend said. "Say, so am I. Let's go get us a drink!"

Ray Baker
Nashville, Tenn.
Record Producer

The Secret of Long Life

A man, well along in his eighties, was out in his garden shoveling manure, just making it fly. A stranger came along the road, watched him for a while and then remarked on how hard he was working. "How old are you?" he asked.

"I'm eighty-six," the old man said.

"You sure do look younger than that," the stranger said. "To what do you attribute your long life and health?"

"I have never tasted a drink of whiskey," the old man said.

About then a terrific commotion erupted in the house.

"What's that?" the stranger inquired.

"Oh, pay no attention to that. It's just Pa on one of his periodic drunks."

Loyal Jones

Dogs and Hunting

Laughter's never an end, it's a by-product.
—STRUTHERS BURT

Hunting

I've never gone coon hunting but I especially like coon hunters, and I especially like the story about an old guide out in the mountains here who was showing some coon hunters around. They came to a hollow tree and they thought there was a coon up there so they cut the tree down and a bear came out! They all left in a hurry and old Uncle Zeke didn't seem to be with them. They stopped when they saw the bear wasn't following and they said, "What's happened to Uncle Zeke?" They all thought that the bear had had a good meal of Uncle Zeke and they were so sorry; but knew they'd have to go tell his widow and they couldn't decide on who should tell her. They went to his home and knocked on the door, and Uncle Zeke showed up!

"Uncle Zeke, are you here?" they said.

"Well, what are you looking at?"

"How'd you get here?"

"Well, I just ambled along with the dogs!"

Dr. W. Gordon Ross
Berea, Ky.

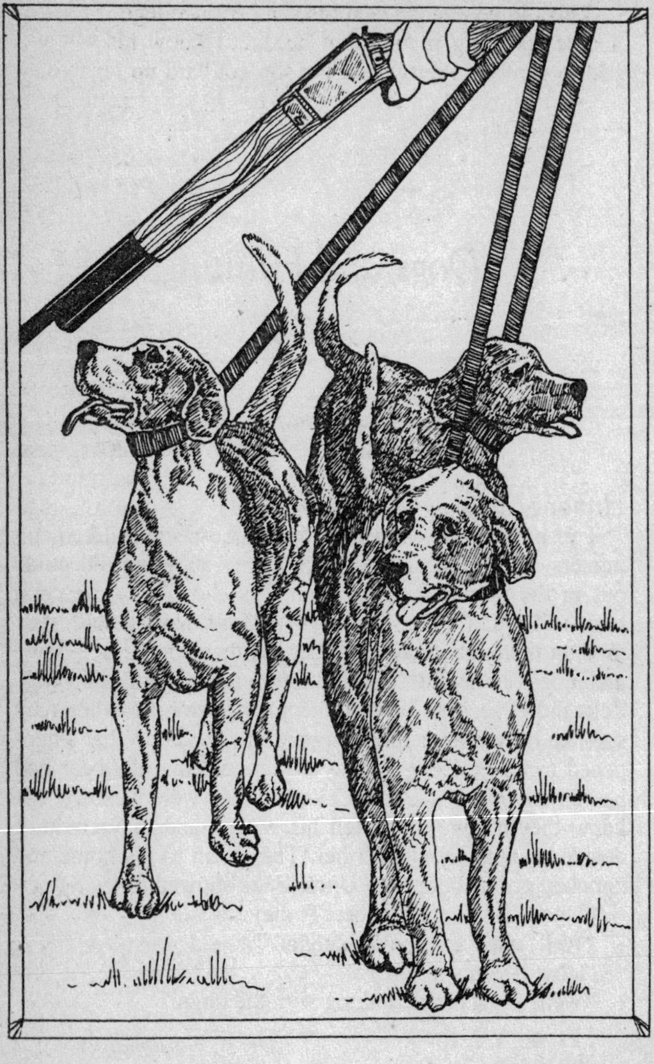

Old Blue Learns to Read and Write

This old gentleman sent his son off to college, gave him a little spending money, but he didn't know his son was bad to gamble. Pretty soon the son got hard up for money, so he dreamed up a little story to milk some more funds from his dad.

He wrote his father and said, "Dad, this college does a lot of experimental work with animals and after I told them about Old Blue, why, they believe they could teach him to read and write. If you'll send him on the train, with about $300, I'll enroll him in the school." The old man thought it would be fun to have a dog that could read and write, so he sent Old Blue to his son, along with $300, which was gambled away pretty quick.

So the son wrote home again, "Dad, Old Blue has learned to read and write. He's a whiz! Fact is, he's so good they think they can teach him to talk. Please send $300 more." The boy's father got to thinking about the fun he'd have showing that dog off down at the store, so he sent the $300. The boy hit a streak of bad luck in his gambling, so in about three weeks he was broke. He wrote home one more time.

"Dear Dad," he wrote, "Old Blue is doing so good, they even think they could teach him to sing. Send $300 and I'll enroll him in the music school."

By the time the son was supposed to come home for Christmas, his father had boasted all around about his wonder dog that could talk and sing. The whole county turned out with him to meet the train, and when his son stepped off the train, the father ran up to him. "Son, where's Old Blue?"

"Dad," the boy said, "wait till we get in the pickup. I'll tell you all about it."

"But, son," the father protested, "everybody wants to see Old Blue ... your aunts and uncles, cousins, neighbors. Where is he?"

"I'll tell you when we get in the pickup. Come on."

When they were alone in the pickup the frustrated father said, "Now, son, tell me about Ole Blue."

"Well," the boy said, "Old Blue was doing well with his reading and writing, and his talking and singing. And then this morning we were getting ready to leave. I was standing there shaving and Ole Blue was sitting on the commode reading the *Wall Street Journal*. He looked up at me and said, 'Do you think your old man is still fooling around with that young schoolteacher?' I tell you, Dad, it made me so mad I just took that razor and cut his throat with it."

The old man said, "Son, are you right sure he's dead?"

> *Chet Atkins*
> *Luttrell, Tenn.*
> *(As told by "Gentleman" Jim Reeves)*

Carbolic and the Cat

My favorite story was about a foxhound named Carbolic. Riley Wilson told it, said Carbolic was owned by Colonel Walker, the man who developed Walker hounds.

Colonel Walker had an annual fox hunt. One of the first arrivals was a Colonel Bradley, who sat sipping a mint julep with Colonel Walker, who told him, "Ed, I've got the greatest dog I've ever bred." And just then a big yellow hound ambled up and laid down on the veranda. Colonel Bradley remarked on what a fine-looking dog it was.

"That's the hound I'm talking about," Colonel Walker said, "that's old Carbolic. No dog ever headed him. He can whip his weight in wildcats. Wait till you see him in action tonight!" But they didn't have to wait. A big tomcat strolled by and Carbolic took after him, across the pasture toward the L&N Railroad tracks, where the hound caught up with the cat. The fight was furious, right in the middle of the tracks, when an express train rounded the curve and made mincemeat of both the dog and the cat.

It happened so fast both colonels were speechless as they walked to the fatal scene.

Colonel Bradley finally said, "Colonel Walker, there's nothing I can say to console you for the loss of your great dog."

Walker was silent until they reached the place where

that speeding locomotive had hit Carbolic and the cat. There was nothing left but hide and hair. "I'll never breed his equal," Walker said, "but I'm not thinking of myself. I'm worried about old Carbolic . . . he had so much *pride*. Through all eternity he'll think that damned tomcat killed him!"

Dr. Eslie Asbury
Carlisle, Ky.

The Wheelchair Case

Now Charlie Lakes, he liked to go out coon huntin'. Charlie, he's from Lexington. I got this information from Brenda Russell, and she got it from Clayton Russell, who got it from his uncle.

But Charlie was out coon huntin' and they treed a coon up a white oak tree. They sawed the tree down and when it fell it split and half of it flopped over and bounced onto Charlie's dog and broke its front legs. A sad story.

Well, the men decided they'd have to shoot the dog, of course. But there's a young lad there, neighbor to Charlie, and he begged for them to give him the dog. He hated to see them shoot that dog. It'd been an awful good dog, you know, very faithful, always got the coon. So they agreed, and gave the boy the dog. They never thought no more about it.

Then about three weeks later, one night, why Charlie woke up in the middle of the night and heard this dog a-barkin'. It sounded like his old coon dog. So he got a light and went outside about the barn. Here this boy was with the dog in a wheelbarrow, a-runnin' a coon. Poor fella, the boy that is, he was plumb wore out. Why, that dog like to run coon so much that the boy had to take him out ever night. Needed a new pair of boots ever month to keep from wearing his legs off.

Dr. John Ramsay
Berea, Ky.

The Skin Board

Tommy, he had this dog. Tommy he's a kinda lazy fellow, you know. He didn't like to do anything unless he had to. Got up late and sat around all evening. That kind of thing. So, it was aggravating for him to go out coon-huntin' and come back in and find he didn't have a skin board the right size to put the skin on. If he got him a big coon, he'd only have him a small skin board and he'd have to stop to make a new big skin board. If he got him a little coon, why the skin board would be too big and small skin wouldn't fit it. They's always a problem.

Now Tommy was smart even if he was lazy, and his dogs were noted for being uncommon smart. He trained them in all sorts of tricks, and jobs, too! Oh, they would roll over, and count, and even multiply. Well, he trained one of the dogs to tree coons the right size for his skin boards. He'd hold up a skin board for the dog before he ever went out.

The dog would then go and get him a coon to fit the skin board.

Well, that worked fine, except that the dog, hit disappeared. And, of course, Tommy worried about him because he'd always been a faithful dog. He finally figured out what happened to him. You know, his wife Carolyn had put the ironing board out on the back porch and Tommy figured that dog was probably out there still lookin' for a coon big enough to fit it.

Now, folks down there around Brasstown, North Carolina, they scoff at that. They just didn't believe that could be the truth. They said that somebody just swiped that dog or he got killed or lost or something like that, you know. But I was telling Bill Sparks about that—he lives out there near Paint Lick, here in Kentucky, runs the slaughterhouse —any of you know him? Plays the banjo and everything, a good fella. I was telling him about Tommy's dog.

"Well, no," he says, "that dog's not lost. It was out looking for a big coon, and it heard there were some big ones up here in Kentucky. So it came up here around Paint

Lick and it's got it a big coon. It's got the coon penned up not far from here cause he's not quite big enough yet and he's feeding him on corn to try to make it grow a little more. Then he'll take him back to North Carolina."

Dr. John Ramsay
Berea, Ky.

The Accordion Dog

When I's a little boy I had this dog my daddy gave me and I didn't want to go to school no more. I wanted to spend all my time playing with that dog. Everywhere I went he went and everywhere he went I went. You couldn't separate us a-tall. Now when I started growing up we went out huntin' together. And he's a pretty fast dog.

Well, we was comin' back in one Saturday afternoon, hit was rainin' cats and dogs, and walking along the state road I was about as wet as Noah during the forty-day rain. Well, this tourister came along driving a big black Cadillac and asked me if I'd like a ride. I told him I'd sure appreciate it. It was okay back in those days to take a ride with a stranger, but I wouldn't do it today. I got in and told my dog to come in with me. Now that tourister, he said, "I'll take you for a ride but I won't take your dog." So I told that tourister that was all right. My dog was fast and he could just run along outside.

So that tourister he started up and he was going about thirty-five miles an hour and says, "How's your dog a-doin'?" And I told him he's right outside the window doin' fine. Well, he went up to fifty-five miles an hour, asked me, "How's your dog a-doin'?" and I told him he's right outside the window doin' fine.

Well, that man he slammed on the brakes, jumped out, and ran around to my side of the car to see if I was a liar. And he seen my dog there. 'Course he didn't much look like a dog, all folded up like an accordion with his tail stickin' out his mouth. He said, "What in tarnation?"

I told him, I said, "Mister, my dog is used to runnin' fast but ain't used to stoppin' that quick!"

Dr. John Ramsay
Berea, Ky.

New Hunter

There was a lady back home who was pestering her husband for staying away from home so much, going deer hunting. He did a lot of hunting.

To satisfy her, he said, "We'll just take you down town and buy you some gear and a gun and you can go deer hunting with me."

They did that; and went out into the woods. Before they started out he told her, "Now, just one thing. The men around here are pretty bad about stealing game after it's killed. If you kill one and anybody comes up and tries to take that deer from you, you get your gun up and protect it!"

And, sure enough, pretty soon along came what she thought was a deer, and she up and shot it; down it went. She looked up and there came a man around the bend running . . . She got her gun up and said, "Just a minute, you're not going to get my deer!"

He said, "Lady, could I at least get my bridle and saddle?"

Glen Baker
Fairmont, W.Va.

The Hunting Horse

A friend of mine invited me over to his farm to hunt birds one time. Our property was separated by a large lake, so I rowed over to his house by raft, to save time. It was several miles around by road. When I got there I was surprised that he didn't take any dogs to show us where the quail were. "We'll just use my hunting horse," he said. "He ain't all that bad."

And I'll say he wasn't! Why, I'd never seen anything like it. That horse could smell out a covey of birds quicker'n a dog. He never made a false point. He knew how to hold them until we were ready to shoot and when my friend made just a small clicking noise with his mouth, that horse would charge in and flush them up. I had a lot of birds on my property I wanted to hunt, but I was never much for dogs.

My friend said he wouldn't sell the horse, but he'd loan him to me any time. One day I went to get him for a hunt, told my friend I'd just row the horse over to my place by raft, save going all the way around. "Ah, I wouldn't do that, if I was you. I'd keep that horse away from that lake." When I asked why, he said, "You get him down on that lake, you'll never get him away. He'd rather fish than hunt any day, and he ain't all that bad at it!"

Ray Baker
Nashville, Tenn.

Interpretation of Humor

DR. W. GORDON ROSS

I'm here to destroy humor. When you analyze, you destroy. That's what they call the "paralysis of analysis." Now, I'm going to start on a very sour note. Not everybody believes in humor or thinks it is important, and I'd like to give you a few quotations:

> The loud laugh bespeaks the vacant mind.
> Laughter is the hiccup of a fool.

A name some of you will remember is Wyndham Lewis. He said:

> Laughter is the mind sneezing.

But the "best" example I have of criticism of laughter is from Lord Chesterfield, an urbane man, a very polished, high-grade, upper-class man. He wrote in a letter to his son:

> Loud laughter is the mirth of the mob, who are only pleased with silly things. For true wit, or good sense,

never excited a laugh since the creation of the world. (That's a long time!) A man of parts and fashion is therefore only seen to smile, but never to laugh.

If I were to tell you three little stories, would you be able to tell if they were (1) humor, and (2) Appalachian? Some of you, I am sure, pronounce it Appalachian. I'll give you a poem to remind you how to pronounce it:

> *Snake, said Eve,*
> *If you try to deceive,*
> *I'll throw this apple-atcha.*

Here's the first little tiny story from eastern Kentucky:

There was an old gentleman from the hills who made one of his rare trips to town. Some of his friends found out that he had never tasted a banana, so they said, "Uncle Jeff, have a banana."

"No, thank you," he said.

They kept on: "Why don't you eat a bite, Uncle Jeff, you might like it."

He said, "I got more *wants* now than I can satisfy!"

The second story concerns another old gentleman from the back country:

Well, there was this old gentleman, Mr. Wilson, who went with some friends for the first time to a city, where they had a zoo. For a moment they lost him. Then they found him, looking at the giraffe. They said, "Mr. Wilson, what do you think of that?"

He said, "There ain't no such animal!"

My third example is this:

Several years ago a famous historian, James T. Shotwell, spoke here at Berea College. Afterwards one of the students went up and said something to him. Dr. Shotwell turned to me and said, "That's delightful. That's the finest compliment I ever got." What the student had said, very cheerfully, was: "Dr. Shotwell, that was a fine speech. You put the fodder where the calves could reach it."

Now let's go back over those stories. The first one is humor and it is Appalachian. But the laughter is not on Uncle Jeff. The laughter is on the people who heard it. They were laughing at themselves. (One of the important ingredients of humor is the ability to laugh at yourself.) Here is the analysis and this is important: At first they put Uncle Jeff on their level. They thought he would go along with ordinary, unspectacular human nature and accept something that was free.

He, all of a sudden, appeared on a higher level and those people realized, maybe not consciously, that they had made a mistake. His statement was not just humor, it was also a sort of philosophy, an outlook on life. A man who has will-power can change, control some of his possible desires. There's a bit of nobility in that.

Now, the other man—the man and the giraffe—that's a little different. He stayed on the same level. If you have to give it a name, you can call it *naive realism,* naive meaning unsophisticated, elemental, juvenile. (I will give you an example: My daughter, when she was three, went with us on a picnic. A beautiful evening. She looked up at the moon when we got home from the picnic and she said, "The moon came home with us." That's beautiful.)

Mr. Wilson couldn't conceive of seeing such an animal as the giraffe, so we laugh at him from the height of superiority. That's one theory of humor, based on the feeling of superiority, that you are better off than the other fellow. One of the best examples of that, perhaps, is when Mark Twain came back from England and one of his friends said, "Did you see the Prince of Wales?" Mark Twain was offended, maybe unconsciously, so he says: "No, I was out when he called."

The third example, what the young man said to Dr. Shotwell, is not humor. You didn't laugh at it particularly. It is not humor. It is *poetry* . . . mountain poetry. I'll give you an example: Years ago a new flashlight came out that shot a solid beam. A friend of mine wanted to buy some meat. He'd heard about a family down the way toward Hazard that had meat in the smokehouse. "Yes, we can let you have some meat," the lady said and took them out to the smokehouse—it was about sundown—unlocked the door and went in. Then she turned to the man with the flashlight and said, "Squirt your light over this way." I don't believe you could beat that.

When you talk about Appalachia and humor, this subject is bound to come up: laughing at the mountaineer—the outsider's laughing *at* the mountaineer. Of course, that can go both ways, and that is what I call a *corruption of humor.* One of my favorite topics concerns what happens to humor from its beginning in human experience and human life on into the future, because of all the corruption that comes in.

Back when we had milk bottles, a boy from the city, visiting the country, came running in one day, excited. He'd found some milk bottles out in the corner of the yard and he said, "I've found a cow's nest!" So the mountaineer can make fun of the city slicker, too.

There are groups who are laughed at and on some occasions they even encourage it. I think of the Scots, some Scotch people, who sit around thinking up jokes on the stinginess of the Scotch. And there's a certain bit of that in Appalachia.

There's an "inside" joke. I'll give you an example: Somebody asked an old hillbilly back in the sticks, "What do you do when you move?" He said, "Well, it's very simple. I just put out the fire and call the dogs."

I wanted to get Arkansas into this because, of all the

states, I don't think any area has had so much fun poked at it as Arkansas. Nobody seems to understand that, but it might have something to do with the way the word sounds. Arkansas sounds hillbillyish.

And I think there's been no better example of the *inside joke* than all that stuff you've heard about the Arkansas Traveler and the Slow Train Through Arkansas. A lot of Arkansans didn't like that. But others nurtured it.

I think one of the most absurd ways of making fun of the mountaineer has been the Lil' Abner so-called *comic* strip, by Al Capp. I saw one strip and there was a cow in the picture. That cow had a marvelous collection of big, upper front teeth! (Maybe some of you thought cows had upper front teeth!)

One humorist explained to me what there is in the Lil' Abner strip that people laugh at. She said it in an exalted sort of style: "Oh, Lil' Abner . . . *so* handsome, so honest, so generous, so large-hearted, so . . . *stupid!*" That let the cat out of the bag. Or as a friend of mine said, "That lets *part* of the cat out of the bag!"

You see, what people do when they laugh at the hillbilly is laugh from their own supposed level of superiority. They always quote the mountaineer as using ridiculous English, poor grammar and all of that. That's not always true. I've known mountaineers who used excellent English. An example:

> There was a little judge in the Ozarks—a little judge. I mean, a judge of a little circuit in a little town with a little courthouse. Everything was little. There was a lawyer from another area who wanted to impress this judge. He said, "Your Honor, may I tell you the truth?"
>
> This little hillbilly mountaineer judge said, "I am not accustomed to denying that privilege to members of the bar, if they care to use it."

You can't beat that for rising to the occasion.

Now, going a little further, would you be able to tell the

difference between a German joke, an English joke, and an Appalachian joke?

I'll tell you a story that happened in Germany. I'm not going to say whether it's German humor, but it happened there:

> In Cologne, Germany, there is one of the most massive Gothic cathedrals in all of Europe. It is huge! Well, an American tourist was being driven around Cologne in a taxi. He saw a building and asked the taxi driver what it was. "That's city hall," replied the driver.
>
> "How long did it take to build it?"
>
> "Oh, I think four years."
>
> "In America," the tourist said, "we could build that in two."
>
> They passed another building and the tourist asked what it was.
>
> "Oh, that's the opera house."
>
> "How long did it take to build it?"
>
> "Six years."
>
> The tourist said, "In America we could build that in two and a half years."
>
> Well, they finally got to the Cologne Cathedral and this tourist, who was not too sophisticated, said, "What is that?"
>
> The taxi driver said, "I don't know. It wasn't there last night!"

Now I suppose we've all heard the yarn about the British lacking a sense of humor. That's the biggest fake yarn I've ever heard. It's true that sometimes they have stories we don't understand. I learned to like this story (but some Americans don't get it):

> A telephone operator called a number and said, "You have a call from Wembley."
>
> "From where?"
>
> She said, "From Wembley . . . *W* as in Wellington

 . . . *E* as in Eleanor . . . *M* as in Martineau . . ."

    "*M* as in *what?*" (See, I told you that you wouldn't get it!)

I heard a story that I almost don't believe, of a group of people who were on the bank of a stream that had alligators in it. And one boy fell in and was caught by an alligator. The boys on the shore laughed at the boy caught by the alligator! I suppose social customs can dictate certain types of behavior anywhere in the world. But, anyway, this story seems to say that you can learn to laugh at anything. If that's true, then that is a basis of what I said about the corruption of humor. One of the saddest things in human experience to me is how humor can be corrupted: when you laugh at the misfortunes of other people beyond a certain point, when you laugh from a point of superiority.

There has been an attempt to get at the absolute origin of humor in human experience, and you can try it with a baby under the age of six months.

Try two things to make an infant laugh: one is to make an ugly face or put on a mask, and the other is to hold out something for the child and when he reaches for it, pull it back. But there's a very important addition.

In the first place, you must do it playfully. You must do it with good will. You can overdo it. You can scare the child out of its wits by making too ugly a face. And, if you put out something for the child and pull it away when it reaches for it, and keep on doing that, unplayfully, then you violate the principle of humor. The child won't laugh. Some people are willing to go to the length of saying that there is the fundamental basis for humor: *unthreatening ugliness* and *playful frustration.*

When people use humor for purposes of making fun, making fun of people, laughing at them in a derisive, scornful manner, then something creeps into the situation that is not humor, and humor, to be pure, must retain that playful, non-dangerous attitude.

The playfulness was demonstrated to me in my own

experience as a boy. I was playing with a dog, when I was nine years old, and I was amazed at the way that dog would growl and grab my wrist with his teeth. They were savage-looking teeth but he'd just bear down gently. A famous quotation says, "Pardner, when you say that, *smile!*" See, that dog was threatening to bite me, but he was smiling, which meant he was undangerous.

And this idea of holding out something and then snatching it away, I suppose, is what the old vaudeville actor, Ed Wynn, used to do. He'd come rushing out on stage and say to his stooge: "You stole my wife, you horse thief!" You see, you're going along on this railroad track and then, all of a sudden, you're shifted over to another one without warning. It's the suddenness of that, the unexpectedness of it, that gives it humor. For another example of incongruity we can quote Groucho Marx, who once said, "I'd horsewhip you, if I had a horse!"

So, there are two basic theories of humor which have something to say for them, I believe. They form the foundation of humor: *unthreatening ugliness* and *playful frustration*.

Now I'm going to close with a story I thought I couldn't tell, but Billy Edd and Loyal and some of these have changed my mind. It's an Arkansas story and it goes along with this thought that you must not *assume* anything, especially assume that someone *implied* something else besides what he said:

This has to do with an old fellow who was in very good health, but friends thought they'd like to get him to a doctor and have the doctor examine him and see what it was that made him so healthy. He was seventy-five. Well, the doctor examined him and was impressed. And the doctor said to him, "What did your father die of?"

"I never said he died," replied the man.

"Well, what did your grandfather die of?"

The man said, "I never said he died. As a matter

of fact, he's getting married next Wednesday."

"How old is he?" asked the doctor, and the man replied, "One hundred seventeen years old, and he's marrying a girl of twenty-three."

"Well, why does he want to marry a girl of twenty-three?" asked the doctor.

The man replied, "I didn't say he *wanted* to!"

Jesse James Bailey

Many of the stories in this book were collected from Jesse James Bailey, one of the most colorful men in western North Carolina. He was sheriff of two different counties, Madison and Buncombe, with Asheville as its county seat. Asheville was the home of Thomas Wolfe, the famous novelist, who wrote about Asheville and its people in many of his books, especially the first one, **Look Homeward, Angel.** (Jesse James Bailey claims to have known Tom Wolfe, said he saw him riding on the train a lot.)

When Jesse got ready to run for sheriff in Madison County he approached the moonshiners and asked for their support. He said, "Boys, I won't bother you none. Lessen I stub my toe on one of your stills in the middle of the street, I'll not harass you." But they didn't believe him, for one reason because he wouldn't take a drink, and they didn't trust a man who wouldn't drink. So he turned to the dry crowd to get himself elected, especially the good people of the Mars Hill region.

And he won. In 1920.

Then he declared war on the moonshiners. He said, "Boys, I asked for your support and you wouldn't give it,

so I'm gonna tear your little playhouse down." And he did. The copper kettles piled high behind the courthouse at Marshall, North Carolina. He drove the price of whiskey up to $75 a gallon! He was fearless and he was imaginative, he was colorful and he was ingenious, he was tough and he was comical.

Like the time he dressed in women's clothes trying to penetrate a house of ill repute on the outskirts of town. He decked up complete with wig, bra, make-up, dress, and hose. He must have been a sight! When he knocked on the front door a lady looked out a top-floor window and exclaimed, "Who's that big-foot woman down there?"

The madam took one look and said, "That's Sheriff Bailey. One of you ladies go down and let him in." And they did . . . *after* they poured all the moonshine down the commode and flushed it. Jesse said, "I could smell it. They tried to cover it over with lye, but I could smell it." He finally caught them with it, by climbing a tree and getting through a window before they had time to get rid of the moonshine.

Jesse usually got his law-breaker, one way or another.

One time he raided a still but the man running it got away. But in his haste, he left his gun behind. Jesse took the gun to the nearest neighbor's house and, holding it reverently, said, "Ma'am, could you loan me a blanket? We've killed a man and we need something to wrap him up in." The lady took one look at the gun and exclaimed, "Oh, dear, you haven't shot John Brown!" (Not his real name.) Jesse swore out a warrant for John Brown, locked him up, returned the blanket to the lady, saying, "Thank you kindly. I guess he wasn't quite dead after all."

The following are a few of the dozens of stories told by Jesse James Bailey about his sheriffing days in Madison County. The stories were taped, so in most cases the quotes are his exact words, though even these few had to be edited considerably.

—BILLY EDD WHEELER

The Telephone Bush

I was pretty bad after the moonshiners. They'd try to beat me and I'd try to beat them. 'Course, I wouldn't harm one in any way, or shoot him, unless he shot at me.

There was two fellows way back right next to the Tennessee line, between Unicoi County and Madison County, place called Devil's Fork. They'd bought 'em enough copper and built a brand-new still. I got on to it. I had informants, you know, sort of like the C.I.A. I found out when they was going to run. Nobody in those days ever stilled at night . . . afraid we'd slip up on 'em . . . so I went in there before daylight, about four in the morning. And directly these boys come, looking around everywhere. They was working and getting ready. They had a little sign on a bush there . . . just made with a pencil, and the sign says "Rabbit Hill Church."

After they got their still fired up, they stepped back to admire it, the shiny new copper just a-gleaming. They was right proud of it. One says to the other, "Boy, ain't that purty! I wish old Sheriff Bailey could just see that one time." The other one says, "Yeah, I do too. What would he say?" The other one says, "I don't know, but I'm going to call him up." He went over there to a little bush, got hold of it and started grinding this bush like a telephone crank. Says, "Give me Sheriff Bailey!"

I just stepped out and says, "Right here, son." That fella like to have fainted.

My Goodness, Sheriff, Is That a Still?

To show you how cunning they are . . . how quick they can fix up an alibi . . . I was watching a still one morning and it was cold. It was way up here between Big Pine Creek and Little Sandy Mush. He'd picked up some dry chestnut limbs, a big armful, and he come right on down to the still and kicked the snow off a bit and throwed his wood down right in front of it. I knew the fella, he was an old friend of mind, but I was surprised to see him five miles from home.

So I just stepped out of where I was hid and he looked up. I thought he was going to run, but he didn't. I said, "Good morning, George."

And he said, "Why, good morning, Sheriff."

I walked hastily down to him and said, "George, what are you doing here this morning, and it so cold?"

He says, "Well, I started to fox hunt."

"My golly," I says. "Where's your dogs?"

He says, "Well, I tell you, I was going across the hill down to Frank Reynolds's."

I said, "Well, George, what was you gonna do with that wood?"

George says, "I was going to build me up a little fire and warm my clothes and dry my shoes."

I said, "George, you wasn't gonna build a fire under this *still* here, to warm your feet by, were you?"

George says, "Sheriff, Lordy mercy no, is there a *still* here?"

I said, "George, what's this?" And I pointed at the still.

And he says, "Sheriff, is that a still?"

I says, "It sure is!"

He says, "Why, I swear that's the first one I ever seen in my life, and if I'd have knowed that was here, I wouldn't have stopped for a thousand dollars!"

I said, "George, I've got a good notion to knock you down... to look at me and think I'd believe a story like that! I'm going to let you tell that to the judge."

And I did. And the judge didn't believe it, either.

Old Pa

There was a farmer down there in Madison County had a nice place with lots of birds on it. He was an old man, like I am now, but he had a young boy that looked after everything.

Some hunters went down there and said they wanted to hunt some birds, and the boy said, okay, he'd take them down in the field and let them kill some birds. One of the hunters said, "We'd better go get our dogs."

"Did you bring dogs?" the boy asked. The hunters said

yes. The boy said, "Well, we ain't been using dogs. People coming here to hunt have been using old Pa. He can scent a gang of birds better than any dogs."

The hunters didn't believe that, but they hated to dispute the boy's story, so he went in and got the old man and they went hunting. By golly, the old man would find a covey of birds, get the fellas all set, and he'd shoo them up. They just killed a passel of birds all along. Had a good hunt.

Next year they decided to go back. So they got together, got their guns and got in the car, left their dogs to save the trouble, and went back to the same place. The same boy was there. "We've come back to hunt," they said.

The boy says, "All right, but where's your dogs?"

Hunter says, "Why, we never brought no dogs. Last year your dad served that purpose. We was well pleased and decided to use him again."

Boy says, "Well, didn't you hear what happened to old Pa? Pa got to running rabbits and we had to shoot him!"

Left-Handed Squirrel Hunter

Asheville fellas, they all liked to go down to Madison County, back up in the Laurels where there was good squirrel hunting. One time they went there, asked permission, and the old man says, "I'm going to send my boy in with you to show you where to hunt."

On the way in, as they went along, the boy gathered him up some rocks. Filled his pocket full. One of the hunters asked him about that and he said, "I always hunt with rocks instead of a gun."

Well, that astounded those fellas. Directly they see a squirrel. Hunter says, "Let me get him!"

Boy says, "No, now, just hold on and I'll get him for you." He reached in his pocket with his left hand, pulled out a rock, and he flung that ole rock and knocked that squirrel out dead as a hammer. He went and picked him up, went down a little further, seen another squirrel. Old boy reached in and got his rock and he whanged down . . . knocked that one out.

Well, these hunters was kind of dumbfounded. They

said, "Son, I was noticing, when you're killing your squirrels you always use your left hand. Why is that?"

Boy says, "Well, Pa won't let me use my right hand. It tears the meat up too bad!"

23,00 Prescriptions

There was people, even dry people, who thought liquor would cure anything to ingrown toenails. And they was honest about it. They'd come to my sheriff's office and want a little liquor to put in camphor, and I wouldn't hesitate to give them some.

But it got so it was annoying me.

The liquor was down in the jail cell and my office was in the courthouse, so it annoyed me so, and took so much of my time, that I appointed a certain day to pour them out all the liquor I had. Here they come, all of 'em lined up with their prescriptions. And their camphor. I'd never give anybody liquor without that in it. I did it myself, I didn't trust them. I'd break it up and put it in their bottles and then pour the liquor in.

I gave away over fifty gallons of liquor there in an hour. It made me drunk. I had to go home and go to bed.

A doctor in those days couldn't demand that you give a patient whiskey, but they could ask nicely and write you a prescription. But I knew the racket, I'd been through it, you know. So I got so I'd take all them doctor's prescriptions and throw them in a desk drawer. I knew someday I was going to make me a scrapbook. I'd just throw them in there. And I think when I went out of office, I had 23,000!

Close to Getting Hung

They had this fellow they's gonna hang . . . had public hangings, you know, in those days . . . brought him out on the scaffold. The sheriff had done put the rope around his neck and pulled the hood down, when the fire alarm sounded.

The sheriff counted the alarms and it was right near his house or, it developed, it *was* his house. It was a little town. Everybody loved the sheriff, so they all tore out to

fight the fire. Left the man standing there on the scaffold
... they hadn't pulled the trigger yet. He just stood there.
He didn't know what was happening, of course, being
blindfolded that way.

Directly, before the crowd got back, a stranger came
along and looked up there, said, "What are you doing up
there?"

The man could see a little bit looking down from under
his hood cap. He very calmly said, "I've been working for
this moving picture company. I get $100 an hour, and I
been here an hour already. But I'm getting tired. Don't you
want the job?"

The stranger, sort of a hobo we'll call him, said, "Yessir, I'd like to have it!"

"Well, come on up here," the victim said. "They don't
care who it is. Just lift this cap off my head and untie my
hands."

The victim took the rope from around his neck and put it
around this guy's neck, pulled the hood down over the
guy's head, and took off running. In his haste he didn't do
a good job in tying the knot. So the fire was over and
everybody remembered their fellow they's fixing to hang
... the sheriff did. He run back down there, him and the
crowd. There was the prisoner with the rope and the hood
still on.

The sheriff climbed up on the scaffold, and without
saying a word he just walked over and pulled the trigger,
you know. That man fell down through there so far and so
hard, but the former victim had tightened the rope so
loosely that it didn't break his neck. It just pulled his head
up and skinned his nose and jerked the old cap off.

The man looked around and saw all this crowd, and he
said, "Looky here, folks, don't you know you're gonna *kill*
somebody one of these days in this-here moving picture
business?"

And with that he kicked that hood and walked away, out
from under that scaffold and on off down the road.

And that's how close he came to getting hung.

Mortgage on Hogs

When I was first elected sheriff, a man defaulted on a mortgage he had given on some hogs, so he had to go before the court. The court ordered me to go out and get the hogs; there were ten of them.

I went over there and it was rough country back then. I told the man that I had come for his mortgaged hogs. He said, "Let's go and catch them."

We got down into some woods there, and he said, "Be right quiet. Don't make any noise."

I said, "What kind of hogs are these that we have to be so quiet?"

"Why, they're groundhogs," he said.

The Lesson

Way back before the Civil War, and after, horse stealing was punishable by death in this state. By golly, they got one of my old ancestors, one of my old uncles for horse stealing, sentenced him to death over there in Madison County . . . that was before I was sheriff.

They got the scaffold all fixed and a big crowd came to see him hang. The sheriff says to him, as he walked out on this platform that he had to go out on to get to the scaffold, sheriff says, "Uncle Jess . . ." (I was named after him, by the way) " . . . Uncle Jess, as we walk there, now, you take it slow and easy."

Old Uncle Jess says, "I don't know how easy I'm going to take it, but it's going to be *awful* slow."

So they got him out there and the sheriff put the rope around his neck, said to him, "Uncle Jess, if you've got anything to say to these good people of Madison County, you've got that privilege, you're at liberty to do it publicly."

My uncle, he looked out over that great throng of people, you know, all standing around looking up. And he says, in a very feeble voice: "You know, this sure is going to be a lesson to me!"

The following story about Eleanor Roosevelt, a distinguished
and esteemed First Lady whose great works and accomplish-
ments are well known, is included not to denigrate her or to
show lack of respect, but because it was one of Jesse James
Bailey's best received stories. I think his referring to her as
"Old Lady" was more a term of endearment than anything, so
we include it as he told it.—Billy Edd Wheeler

Old Lady Roosevelt

After I was sheriff in Asheville I worked for the
railroad . . . had a wonderful experience. I was chief of
what was known as the Railroad Detectives. It was the
duty of railroad officers, when some very important person
was traveling, to travel with them. If it was the President
or the Vice President, or some big senator, the head man
had to go with them, and in this case it was me. But you
didn't let them know who you were, or anything. You just
kept them in sight.

In this instance it was Old Lady Roosevelt, Mrs. Frank-
lin D. Roosevelt. She'd been down here to Salisbury to
address students at Livingston College there, which was a
colored college. That was the thirties, right at the height of
the integration controversy, so when she made application
at the hotel to stay all night, why, the hotel turned her
down. Said they's full up, or something like that.

Well, she'd finished her activities there, making this address, and, well, there wasn't nothing for her to do but get
on the train and go back to Washington. It was about ten
o'clock that night. A train was due in called the Crescent
Limited, a high-class train, but back then they didn't have
nothing but the old-timey Pullmans. You know, they didn't
have bedrooms and drawing rooms and roomettes like they
do now. The only reservation she could get was a lower
berth in this old-time Pullman. Reservations was tight
then. War was breaking out. People traveling.

I was assigned that duty of being close to her, sort of
being in shape to take care of her, or to testify to anything
happening. So, I run into Tom Wolfe. I knew him, and me
and him traveled a bit together then. I'd be on these trains

and Tom would, too. He was on that train that night, going out of Salisbury to New York or somewhere . . . I don't remember the full incident. Him and me was sitting up near the front of the car, you know, and I hadn't seen him in quite a while and we was having a nice friendly chat.

Well, Old Lady Roosevelt came in to take her berth, and retired. She hadn't much more than retired when an old drunk, in the berth above her, got to making noises . . . coughing, being boisterous, disturbing her. So she took her parasol, with a metal tip, and jabbed up from the bottom of that berth. It was metal, too. She bang-bang-banged away. Made a right size of a noise. She slowed him up for a bit, about ten or fifteen minutes.

Directly, he cut loose again, hawking and a-gagging, talking to himself up there worse than ever. Well, she takes her parasol and bangs again. He didn't quieten down this time. He leaned over, pulled the curtains open in her berth, says, "Nothing doing, lady. I got a good look at you when you got on the train!"

Funeral

This old man, Uncle Ephraim, died and they were going to bury him up there on the line between Madison County, North Carolina, and Unicoi County, Tennessee, at a place called Devil's Fork. The only way to get Uncle Ephraim to the cemetery was on a sled, and it was rough and rugged. They got him ready and put him on a sled, and started out for the church which was about four miles up the mountain. Henry, Uncle Ephraim's son, was driving the team of mules, and several of his friends came along. About halfway there, they got tired and the mules got tired, and they stopped at the house of a moonshiner, and they all had a few nips, including Henry. Then they went on toward the cemetery, but the farther up they went the rougher and steeper the road was, but nobody was feeling any pain because of the whiskey.

Some other people who knew Uncle Ephraim came in from the Tennessee side and were waiting for them to get there. One fellow said to his wife, "I'm going to go over and express my sympathy to Henry on the loss of his father."

So he went over and met Henry and said, "Henry, I sympathize with you on the loss of your father. He was a good old man. I'm sorry you lost him."

Henry turned around and looked and said, "I'll be damned if we *ain't* lost him!" He'd slid off about a mile back.

Couldn't Tell Head from Tail

There was this show, a circus, that was moving by wagon, coming across from Flag Pond, Tennessee, by way of Devil's Fork in Madison County. They had several wagons and one or two turned over and these animals got out. One pretty good-sized elephant got away and ran off. They sent for me to come and help catch the animals. Everybody was afraid of them.

I went over to Aunt Polly's house where I heard the elephant might have been. Now, Aunt Polly had never seen an elephant, not even a picture of one.

When she saw me coming, she ran out and said, "Sheriff, that low-down thing went out there in my garden and took its old tail and pulled up all of my cabbages. I just never seen an animal act like that."

I said, "Aunt Polly, what did that elephant do with those cabbages he pulled up?"

"Sheriff," she said, "you wouldn't believe it if I was to tell you!"

There's been some good stories on them Madison County people. They had a lot of humor about them. They're my people.

I loved them and they loved me.

If I could make any money, I'd be there yet. But I can't make no money in Madison County.

Miscellaneous Humor

Laughter is the shortest distance between two people.
— VICTOR BORGE

Troublesome Monkey

A woman in east Tennessee ordered a monkey for a pet, but after several months it became wild and troublesome. She went to see the veterinarian about it. Right away he said, "My advice to you is to take him to the zoo down in Knoxville." She said she would

When the vet saw the lady a few days later, he asked, "Did you take your monkey to the zoo?"

"Oh, yes," she replied, "and we had so much fun I'm going to take him to the movies next Saturday."

Dr. Charles Harris
Berea, Ky.

Skinny Dippers

A woman who lived close to the swimming hole called the sheriff one day and said, "I'm just shocked. A bunch of boys are down there swimming without a stitch on! I want you to come out here and do something about it."

The sheriff drove out, went up on her porch, and knocked. The woman came to the door. "Where is it that you can see them boys from?" he asked.

"Up yonder in my bedroom," she said. So he followed her up to her bedroom, went over to the window and looked down at the swimming hole.

"Why, I can't see anything from here because of the bushes around the hole," he said.

The woman replied, "Oh, you have to get up on this now by the way yer a-talkin' it's not who I's a-wantin'!"

Loyal Jones

Wrong Number

One day I answered the phone, and the voice at the other end said abruptly, "Whosiz?"

"With whom did you wish to speak," I said, being an English major.

There was a long pause and then, "I kin tell ye right now by the way yer-a-talkin' it's not who I's a-wantin'!"

Loyal Jones

Fire in the Kitchen

A woman moved from Kentucky to Dayton, Ohio. One day a fire started in her house, and she called the fire department. The following conversation ensued:

"Hello, I've got a fire out here in my house."

"Okay, where is it?"

"It's in the kitchen."

"I mean, how do we get to it?"

"Well, you come in off the back porch or through the living room, either one."

"No, I mean, how do we get from here where we are to you out where you are?"

"Ain't you got one of them big red trucks?"

Loyal Jones

It Might Be Taller Than It Is Long

A fellow was walking by a neighbor's house one day when he saw a strange sight. His neighbor had leaned a long stackpole up in a tree and was attempting to climb the pole with a measuring stick to find out how tall it was.

"Why don't you just lay it down on the ground and measure it?" the man asked, trying to be helpful.

"Because I don't want to know how long it is. I want to know how tall it is," he answered.

Dr. Rodney Bates
Stanton, Ky.

The Hired Girl

A girl from the country went into town to get a job and found one with a lawyer's family in town who were pretty high-faluting folks. The girl cooked, cleaned the house, and did the wash and that sort of thing. The daughter of the family got engaged to a young man up the street who hung around the house with the daughter quite a bit.

One day the lady of the house called to the hired girl, "Have you seen my daughter's fiancé?"

"No, she ain't put it in the wash yet."

Loyal Jones

Of Outhouses and Cherry Trees

One time at Halloween, Jack Barlow and I just couldn't find enough mischief and tricks to pull on people, but we done our best, and the last thing we did was to push over the two-holer out behind our house. It was a cold crisp night and the frost was on the pumpkin. That outhouse made one heck of a splash when it rolled into the Big Coal River. I figured that by morning it would be floating down the Kanawha, heading for the Ohio and eventually the mighty Mississippi itself. Now that was a nice piece of work!

Next morning Pap snatched me out of bed by my ear. He looked awful cross, like he'd tangled with a couple of chain saws and lost. He said, "Billy, I'm gonna ask you a question and, by grabs, I want the truth. Did you and Barlow push over our outhouse last night . . . into that cold, cold river?" I knew I was in real trouble, but I made a historic stab at a way out.

I said, "Well, Daddy, just like George Washington . . . I can't tell a lie. Yes, sir, we did." With that, he took off his belt and commenced to blister my sitting-down place pretty good with it. I protested: "When George Washington cut down the cherry tree and told the truth about it, his daddy didn't whip him!"

Pap said, "Yeah, and I don't reckon George's daddy was *in* that cherry tree when he chopped it down, neither!"

Billy Edd Wheeler

Advice
Don't ever hit a man who's chewing tobacco.

Dr. John Ramsay
Berea, Ky.

Fourteen Kids and One A-Comin'
There was this man and woman who had fourteen children, and the man swore to a neighbor that if his wife got pregnant again he'd shoot himself. Well, she did, and he took his revolver and went out behind the barn. The neighbor came by inquiring about him. His wife told him that she'd seen her husband go out behind the barn with his gun.

The neighbor rushed behind the barn and found the man sitting on a stump whittling with his gun laid beside him.

"I was afraid you were going to shoot yourself," the neighbor said.

"Well, I was a-going to," the man said, "but I got to worrying that I might be executing an innocent man."

Bob Sears
Somerset, Ky.

Progress

A rural woman went into town to see if she could get a loan to build a bathroom in her house. She had never been in a bank, so she was nervous. She got right to the point with the bank president. "I want to borrow a thousand dollars to put a bathroom in my house."

The president was cautious and responded, "I don't believe I know you. Where have you done your business before?"

"Oh, out back in the pine thicket," she replied.

Becky Nelson
Berea, Ky.

Practical Way

A country fellow was going through town dragging a long chain. When he went by a store, the merchant called out, "Hey, mister, why are you pulling that chain?"

The man replied, "Because it's easier than pushing it."

Loyal Jones

Legacy

Two fellows met on the street. "Did you hear that Bill Johnson died last night?" one said, speaking of a wealthy late citizen.

"How much money did he leave?" the other one asked.

"All of it," the other responded.

Loyal Jones

Athletics

There was this country boy in college who desperately wanted to get on one of the athletic teams, but the truth was that he wasn't too good at sports. After trying for two years, he finally was accepted to the football team as a third-stringer. At the very first game, he was sitting on the bench watching the plays when someone threw a long pass, hit him in the nose—and broke his finger.

Dr. John B. Stephenson
Berea, Ky.

Parentage

A woman in western North Carolina named her child Morphine. She said she had heard that Morphine was the product of a wild poppy. "Her poppy was about the wildest scoundrel that ever passed through here."

Hon. Felix Alley
Cashiers, N. C.

Riddle

Question: What is the difference between the Prince of Wales, a bald-headed man, a young monkey and an orphan child?

Answer: The Prince of Wales is an heir apparent; the bald-headed man has no hair apparent; the monkey has a hairy parent; and the orphan child ain't got ary parent.

Hon. Felix Alley
Cashiers, N. C.

Simple Logic

A man came home after working late one night and found his wife in bed and his best friend hiding in the closet.

"Why, John, what are you doing in there?" he asked.

"Well, Bert," his friend answered. "Everybody has to be somewhere."

Loyal Jones

Letter

Mom wrote me a letter. Back in the days when she grew up people didn't get to go to school much like they do now. She did the best she knew how in putting things over in writing:

"Dear Son,

"Just a few lines to let you know I'm still alive. I am writing this slowly because I know that you can't read fast. You won't know this house when you

come home. We've moved. About your father. He
has a lovely job. He has 500 people under him. He is
cutting grass in the cemetery. There was a new washing machine in the new house when we moved in,
but it wasn't working too good. Last week I put 14
shirts in it and pulled the chain and I haven't seen
them since. Your sister Elsie had a baby last week. I
haven't found out yet whether it's a boy or a girl, so I
don't know whether you are an aunt or an uncle.
Your uncle Arnold drowned yesterday in a vat of
corn whiskey out on the side of Bates Ridge. Some
of the boys dived to save him but he fought them off
bravely. We cremated the body and it took three days
to put out the fire. I went to the doctor last week and
your father came with me. The doctor put a tube in
my mouth and told me not to speak for ten minutes.
Your father offered to buy it off of him. It rained
twice last week, first for three days and then for four
days. On Monday it was so windy one old hen laid
the same egg three times. We got a letter from the
undertaker and he said that if the last installment
wasn't paid on your grandma's funeral within 7 days,
up she comes. I would have sent you 5 dollars but I
don't seal the envelope.

   "Love, Mom"

                                    Lewis Lamb
                                    Paint Lick, Ky.

Success

A man made a fortune in the coal business in eastern
Kentucky, and he and his wife decided to move to Lexington. They bought a nice house and settled down to a life of
leisure. One evening his wife suggested that they go out to
a good restaurant she had heard about. He agreed to go,
but after they got dressed, his wife said:

"Now, Herbert, I want to talk to you before we go. All
your life you've scrimped and saved and run around trying
to get the best deal on everything and trying to talk the

price down on everything you bought. As you well know, we've got so much money that we can't ever spend it. Tonight I want you to go into that restaurant like you are somebody and order whatever you want from the menu without studying it for an hour to see what the best bargain is. I don't want you going in there and acting like you can't afford a good meal."

So they went to the restaurant, got a good table, looked over the menu, which was pretty big, with a lot of things on it that neither of them understood.

When the waiter came and asked what they wanted, old Herbert leaned back and said, "Just bring me about fifty dollars' worth of scrambled eggs."

Loyal Jones

City Slicker and Country Boy

A country fellow got on a bus and sat down by a slick-looking fellow from the city. The city fellow looked the country boy over and decided to have some fun and make a little money too.

"Let's play a game to pass the time," he said, "and to make it worthwhile, I'll give you a dollar for every question that you ask me that I can't answer. You give me fifty cents for every question I ask you that you can't answer. And you can ask the first question."

The country boy thought a minute and then asked, "How come there is no pile of dirt on the outside when a rabbit digs his hole?"

The city fellow thought for a while, gave up and said, "Here's your dollar. I don't know. Why isn't there a pile of dirt?"

"Because he starts from the bottom," replied the country boy.

The city man said, "Aha, my question is, how does he get to the bottom?"

"I don't know," said the country boy. "Here's your fifty cents."

Loyal Jones

A Sauce for the Plum Pudding

Years ago an English family moved to Asheville, lived there for six years, and then decided to go back to England, except for the son, who had married and had children, a good job. He decided he'd stay. So his mother, his Aunt Alice and Uncle Herbert, the family, went back home.

Every year at Christmas time his mother sent him his favorite dish, a plum pudding. One year the pudding arrived without a note, and in the box with the pudding was a little jar filled with a grayish-white powder. He and his wife studied that powder... finally decided that it was a dehydrated sauce his mother had sent to use on the plum pudding. So his wife put it in a saucepan, mixed it with water, cooked it, and poured it over that plum pudding, and they ate it. He thought it was pretty good, because his mother had sent it to him, but his wife thought it tasted pretty bland.

A couple of days later they got a note from his mother in England. It said, "Dear son, I hope you enjoyed your Christmas pudding. I suppose Aunt Alice wrote you about Uncle Herbert's passing away. I hope it wasn't too much trouble for you to fulfill his last request... that his ashes be spread over the French Broad River!"

Bob Terrell
Asheville, N.C.

Choices

At the Craftsman's Fair in Asheville many years ago, two of the women who did crafts stayed in an old hotel near the civic auditorium. One was the daughter of the other, although both were along in years. It was July and an unusually hot one for Asheville. The residents of the hotel had the transoms over their doors open to get circulation. Late at night when everything was settling down, the two woman were heard talking.

The younger one said, "Boy, it sure is hot tonight."

After a bit, her mother replied, "Yeah, it sure is. Why don't we open the door?"

"No, there's some mighty strange men here in Asheville," the daughter said.

A long silence ensued, and then the mother said, "Well, I guess I'd as soon be had as fried."

Suzanne Camp Allen
Rossville, Ga.

The Law

A fellow was driving down the interstate behind a man in an old pickup truck. All of a sudden, the truck started backfiring, giving off clouds of smoke, and bucking and jumping. When the driver pulled over, the man behind pulled over, too, to see if he could help. The driver of the pickup jumped out with two empty milk bottles, ran up on the bank, picked some daisies and clover blossoms, put them in the milk bottles, put one in front of the truck and the other behind. This fellow helped the old man to get his truck running again, and then he asked him about the milk bottles.

"The law says," the man answered, "if you break down on the highway, you have to put flares out."

Loyal Jones

Nothing's Been Happening

This fellow came back home after being away for a spell, saw a neighbor at the edge of town, asked him if there was any news.

"News? Naw, nothing's been happening much that I can think of. Hey, wait a minute, there is one piece of news. Your dog died."

"My dog died? Old Blue? Lordy mercy, how did that happen?"

The neighbor thought a minute. "Well, I reckon it was that burnt horseflesh that killed him."

"Burnt horseflesh!" the fellow said. "Where'd he get into that?"

The neighbor said, "When your barn burned down. Actually, the fire started in your house, then sparks flew over and caught the barn, trapped the horses. The dog ate some horse meat . . ."

"My house burned down!" the fellow cried. "My gracious, how did that happen?"

The neighbor said, "I think it was one of the candles. It must have tilted over during the funeral and set the curtains on fire. Yes, that was probably it."

"F-f-funeral?" the fellow's voice quavered. "At my house? Who died?"

"Your mother-in-law. You see, when your wife ran off with that traveling salesman, it broke her heart and she died. They had a little funeral service at the house and that's when the candles by the coffin caught the curtains on fire, then the house and barn, and them poor horses which Old Blue ate and died. But other than that, nothing much has been happening."

Billy Edd Wheeler

The Paint Job

This backwoodsman rode his mule into town for supplies and when he came out of the general store he noticed that somebody had painted his mule's tail red. Boy, did he get mad. He was fighting mad.

Next to the store was a tavern. The backwoodsman noticed a small empty paint can in the dust in front of the tavern, so he figured that's where the culprit was. He stormed through the door of the tavern, yelled, "Okay, who's the wise guy that painted my mule's tail red?"

A hush fell over the beer-joint crowd as a giant of a man stood up. Took him two minutes to get all the way up, and he looked rough as a cob, dirty, unshaven . . . looked like the type that if you killed him it'd only make him mad. He said, "I did!"

The backwoodsman said, "Well, I just wanted you to know that the first coat's dry." And he smiled and politely stepped back out the door.

Billy Edd Wheeler

Mountain Girl in D.C.

A young mountain woman moved to Washington after she graduated from high school to get a job in an office there. She interviewed for several jobs and was finally hired by Air France, the national airline of France. She started out in a clerical position, but one day the telephone receptionist was ill and she answered it.

"Howdy. This is Air France," she said in a decidedly nasal mountain accent.

An executive rushed out of a nearby office and said in a polished and urbane manner, "No, what you say is 'Hellooo. This is Air Fraance.' "

The young woman said she understood. When the phone rang again, she said, "Hellooo. This is Air Fraance. Kin I he'p ye?"

Loyal Jones

Art

The Woman's Club in a small town was very culture-conscious, and one day the president proposed that they invite a ballet troupe to come to town and do a program. They voted to explore the idea, and the secretary wrote off to a talent agency for information. They discovered that they had only enough money to have one dancer come and demonstrate. So they asked for the ballerina to come on a certain night. The talent agency, however, got things mixed up and sent a stripper.

The town all turned out for the program. They were quite shocked, of course, at the young woman's performance, but no one had ever seen a ballet. Not wishing to show their ignorance, everybody pretended to enjoy the performance, and they left hastily afterwards so that they would not have to discuss it with one another.

The next day the president of the club and her husband were strolling down the street when they met another member of the club. She asked the president, "How did you like the performance last night?"

She hemmed and hawed and said something about its being interesting and perhaps artistic. The woman then turned to the husband and asked him what he thought.

"I'll tell you this much," he responded. "It was no place to take a nervous man!"

Loyal Jones

Full of Corn

Homer Wise loved to hear himself talk. He'd rattle on incessantly about anything and everything, till finally people would hide when they saw him coming. He was running short of an audience. So he started going to the barber shop, where he found he had a trapped audience. He'd jabber on all day while folks were sitting there getting their hair cut. It got to be irritating to the barbers, especially when business started falling off.

One day the head barber made up a story. He said, "Homer, did you hear about the bird singing on the wire?"

Homer thought from the barber's tone of voice he could see something coming, but he couldn't think fast enough to head it off, so he said no.

"Well," said the barber, "this lazy bird found that he could fare pretty well by following these horses around . . . picking the corn out of their droppings. He ate good. Got real fat.

"But one time," the barber said, "after he'd had a pretty good meal, he flew up and lit on a telephone line and started chirping real loud. A boy came along with a BB gun, heard him singing up there, took aim and shot him." Homer looked at the barber, puzzled. The barber said, "The moral of the story is, if you're full of corn, keep your mouth shut!"

It was a pretty corny story, but I guess Homer got the message. He didn't come back to the barber shop for a long time.

Billy Edd Wheeler

Ugly

There was this woman who was so ugly that if you threw her in the lake you could skim ugly for a week.

She was so ugly she couldn't lure a man out of a burning building.

Bill Foster
Florence, Ala.

The Conductor and the Ugly Baby

This slightly drunk passenger on the train looked over at this woman holding her baby and remarked, "Madam, that's got to be the ugliest baby I ever saw in my life!"

The lady took exception, started flailing at the man with her purse, cursing him, yelling, and the man started yelling back. When the conductor came into the car, he rushed down to see what all the commotion was about.

He knew he had to be forceful and take command of the situation right quick. He said, "What's going on here! Let's quiet down, now. You, mister, you just sit down there! And, ma'am, you wait right here. I'll go get a banana for your monkey!"

Billy Edd Wheeler

The Ugliest Girl in the World

I used to date a girl named Beumadean Skelvidge, and she had to be the ugliest girl in the world. She entered a beauty contest at Williamsburg . . . and nobody won!

She went to see the psychiatrist and he made her lay face down on the couch!

One time she was taking a little white duck to the county fair. She stopped at the Blue Bird Cafe to get a co-cola and the waiter hollered at her, "Hey, where are you going with that pig?"

She said, "This ain't no pig, it's a duck!"

"Shut up," he said, "I'm talking to the duck!"

When Beumadean was just a little thing she got separated from her parents out there at Levi Jackson State Park. When she found a policeman, she said, "Do you think we'll ever find my mommy and daddy?"

The policeman said, "I don't know, honey . . . there's lots of places out here for them to hide!"

She was undressing and this Peeping Tom was watching. He reached in and pulled the shade!

Jerry Jones
London, Ky.

Bad Driver

A hitch-hiker got a ride from a fellow in a souped-up Mercury. He had no sooner hit the seat when the driver floorboarded the car and went straight through a red light. The passenger protested, "You oughtn't to do that."

The driver said, "Why, this is the way my brother always drives."

They went on and came to another red light. The driver didn't even slow down, went right on through with cars on the cross street screeching to a stop. The hitch-hiker got a little mad and said, "Look here, you're going to kill us both, driving like that."

Again the driver said, "My brother always drives like this."

They went on down the road, came to another traffic light just as it turned green. The driver threw on his brakes and stopped. The passenger asked, "Why are you going through all the red lights and stopping at this green light?"

The driver replied, "My brother might be coming through."

Ivan Amburgey
Pine Top, Ky.

A Different Kind of Hairnet

A highway patrolman called me once, said, "I've got to tell you what happened to me last night. I was out on Highway 19–23, when I came upon an accident." He said, "Now I've got to go back a little, before the accident, and tell you . . . there's a girl who lives in Enka, name of Sarah Taylor, and she lives with her sister. Neither one is married. Sarah had been to the beauty shop that afternoon and had her hair fixed. Her sister was at work. Sarah got ready for bed but she couldn't find a hairnet. She had to improvise. She searched all over and the closest she could come to duplicating the hairnet was a pair of her nylon underpants. She pulled them down over her hair. It felt just fine, so she went to bed.

"At two o'clock in the morning we called her and told her that her sister had been in an accident and needed her car insurance policy. She didn't know if her sister was half-dead, or what . . . scared her to death. She jumped out of bed, jerked on a robe, grabbed the policy and drove out 19–23 to the accident." He paused and chuckled.

"That was the toughest job I ever had," he said, "standing there looking poor Sarah in the eye, trying to tell her what happened, wondering why she had her pants on on the wrong end!"

Bob Terrell
Asheville, N.C.

Right Zipper, Wrong Man

This man and woman in Asheville had a fight one night . . . a man and wife. Went to bed mad, which they never should have done. Woke up next morning madder still and started off all over again.

Both of them worked, so they were getting ready to go to work. She put on her favorite dress and for some reason she was so mad at him she couldn't reach the zipper. So she backed up to him and just pointed. She didn't talk to him or say anything.

So he grabbed the zipper and zipped it up. And then he

zipped it back down. He thought about how funny that was, so he stood there zipping it up and down until he broke the zipper. Then he had to cut her out of her favorite dress, so you can imagine what that did to her disposition. When she got home from work that afternoon she had *revenge* on her mind. She saw two legs sticking out from under his car, so she knew right then what she was going to do. She went over and got his zipper . . . zip, zip, zip, she ran it up and down a few times. "That'll take care of him," she thought.

She went on in the house and there at the kitchen table sat her husband drinking a cup of coffee!

Bob Terrell
Asheville, N.C.

A Dividing Line

Question: What is the difference between a hillbilly and a son-of-a-bitch?

Answer: The Ohio River.

Bob Gibbs
Richmond, Ky.

Folks Who Talk Funny

Down in North Carolina and north Georgia, a lot of Florida people have bought land and moved in at least for the summer. One fall, about October, a man from the North who had read the *Foxfire* books came down to meet first-hand some of the mountain people he had been reading about. He pulled into a service station for a fill-up and while he was there he inquired of the station attendant, "Where could I find some of these people who talk so funny?"

The attendant looked at him a minute and replied, "You're too late, they've all gone back to Florida for the winter."

Loyal Jones

Granny and the Firing Squad

This is my favorite funeral story: there was a young Marine, home on leave in Asheville from Camp Lejeune. He took his girlfriend out one night, along with another couple, and the four were speeding down Merrimon Avenue. They failed to make a curve and hung that car on a big sycamore tree. Killed the Marine, killed his girlfriend and killed the boy in the back. Only his girlfriend survived.

They sent an Honor Guard up from Camp Lejeune to give that Marine a funeral. He was survived by an aged grandmother and a four-year-old brother. Now, that four-year-old brother was known as a "cusser." Every other word he said was a cuss word.

He and his grandmother went to the cemetery to bury his brother. Before they lowered the casket into the ground, the firing squad off to the side raised their rifles and fired a salute to the fallen hero. It scared the grandmother so bad, she fainted and fell out of her chair, right beside the grave. The little boy looked down at his grandmother, looked over at the firing squad.

"Son of a bitch!" he said. "They've shot Granny!"

Bob Terrell
Asheville, N.C.

Lazy

I had an uncle over in North Carolina who was voted the laziest man in the county. When the committee came out to give him the prize, he said:

"Well, I don't really deserve it, but if you want me to have it, just turn me over and put it in my hip pocket."

Glenn Massey
Manchester, Tenn.

Smart

The other night I ran into Archibald S. Holbrook, a guy I went to high school with, hadn't seen in ten years. Arch used to get into a lot of spelling bees, plus he used to get into a lot of trouble, and he was always broke. But now he was looking great . . . had on a pair of $400 cowboy boots, a nice cowboy hat . . . he'd just stepped out of a brand new Bronco, must have cost a bundle.

I said, "Arch, looks like you're doing pretty good." So he told me about it.

Said he'd just won some money on a quiz show in New York. It was a show where you press a buzzer and he and two other guys pressed at the same time, so they all got a crack at the answer for a $10,000 jackpot.

The emcee asked them to fill in the blank, said, "Old MacDonald had a . . . what?"

The contestant from New York said, "Old MacDonald had a heart attack."

The California guy said, "Old MacDonald had a Mercedes Benz."

Old Arch said, "Old MacDonald had a *farm*," and won, which meant that he had a shot at some additional money.

The emcee said to Arch, "For fifty thousand dollars . . . how do you spell *farm*?"

Arch thought about it a minute. And said, "E-I-E-I-O."

Willie Smyth
Knoxville, Tenn.

Mama Was Blue in the Face

A geologist came to visit this poor dirt farmer, told him he thought there was reason to believe there might be oil or gas on his land and, if he didn't mind, they would drill a hole to find out. He said, "If there's as much oil down there as we think, you'll be a rich man. A very rich man." Of course the farmer told them to go ahead.

They drilled and drilled, going down through dirt and sand, shamrock and shale, limestone . . . down, down, down for a thousand feet. But they never did strike oil or gas. So the geologist said to the farmer, "I guess we struck out. I'm sorry. We'll just put a cap over that deep hole and move on."

The farmer looked over at his outhouse and got a sudden inspiration. "Hey, wait a minute!" he said. "See that outhouse yonder? I've moved that thing several times . . . it's hard work. Why don't you just take that big crane of yours, lift that outhouse up and set it down over that thousand-foot hole? Why, I'd never have to move that thing again!"

The geologist had his men set the outhouse over the hole, and they left. Next morning the farmer's son came running up to the house, very excited, said, "Pap! I'm afraid Mama's dead or something. She's sitting down there in the outhouse, with this strange look. Her face has turned blue, her eyes are bugged out, the blood veins are standing up on the side of her head . . . you better come quick!"

The farmer chuckled, said, "Don't worry, son, your Mama's okay. She just likes to hold her breath till she hears it hit bottom."

Billy Edd Wheeler

The Rusty Dishpan

I was going home down this road . . . it was kinda hot and dusty that day, and when I came to a bend in the road I saw this creek. It looked so nice and cool, and being that close to the road, I thought it would be a good place to take a swim. So I just took off my clothes and piled them on the bank, and I went in there swimming.

After a while that water started getting cold to me and I felt like getting out. But when I looked up on the bank where my clothes was, there set this young woman. Just sitting there grinning at me!

I said, "Please, girl, I'd like to get out and get dressed. Go away!" She just sat there and grinned at me. I said, "Come on, now, go away. I want to get out and put my clothes on." She just grinned.

While I was treading water my foot hit something on the bottom of that creek, and it was a dishpan, kinda old and rusty, but I thought it would do, 'cause I was getting kinda irritated at that grinning girl. I reached down and got that dishpan up, covered myself with it, and went charging up the bank. I said, "Young woman, you know what I think?"

She said, "I guess you think there's a *bottom* in that dishpan!"

Joe Bly
Asheville, N.C.

Setting Poles

Back home, these three boys had been building a fence for their dad. Later on they saw an ad in the paper where the telephone company wanted pole-setters. So they went in and applied for the job. Well, they gave them a job! The first day they worked, when they came in, the boss asked, "How many poles did you set?"

"We set three."

He replied, "You'll have to do better than that. The other crew set forty!"

"Well," they asked, "give us another chance?" So he let them try the second day. Same thing.

So the man said, "We'll just have to let you go; you're just not setting enough poles!"

They said, "All right, we'll just go back and work for Pap; he never objected."

Got to the door and a fellow said to the boss, "By the way, did you notice that they left only five feet of them poles sticking out?"

Glen Baker
Fairmont, W.Va.

The Cat Came Back

The cat was killing the farmer's chickens, and he told his boys to put him in a sack and take him to the river and drown him. So they did. Next morning, there was a scratching at the door; he opened the door and there stood that cat! He told the boys they didn't do a very good job and to take the shotgun this time and shoot him. They took the cat back up in the woods and shot him. Next morning, there was a scratching at the door; he opened it and there stood the cat!

He said, "Well, that's the trouble; sending boys to do a man's job. I'll fix him!" He took him down to the old-fashioned woodyard where they chopped their wood. He laid the cat down on the log and took the axe and chopped his head off. The head fell over here and the body over here. He just let him lie. Next morning, a scratching came at the door and he went and found the cat standing there with its head in its mouth!

Glen Baker
Fairmont, W.Va.

Wrong Ear

I had a fellow working for me on the sawmill one time and he got too close to the saw and he got down and cut his ear off. It fell down into the sawdust pit and he was down looking for it.

When I came by, I said, "What are you doing down there?"

He said, "I cut my ear off and I'm looking for it!"

I said, "Well, I'll help ya!" I got down and found the ear. I said, "Here it is!" He took it and looked at it carefully.

Directly he said, "Keep looking; mine had a pencil behind it!"

Glen Baker
Fairmont, W.Va.

Poverty Warrior

There was a young man here who used to work for the same organization I did, the Council of the Southern Mountains, and he got involved in one of the poverty projects. He bought himself a modest Dodge Dart but he hit a coal truck or it hit him; anyhow, it totaled the Dodge Dart. He got his insurance money and he went out to get another car, but he couldn't afford a new one, so another friend of mine talked him into buying a Buick Electra. It was white and kind of long—this was 1963 and you remember the tail fins and everything—and it was a splendid-looking car! The best part about it, he thought, was it had electric windows! He got lost over in eastern Kentucky and he saw a man standing beside the road, and he kind of tooled over beside him and reached down and lowered the window on that side and asked, "Can you tell me how to get to Lower Grassy?"

The man said, "Yeah, you just go down here a little ways and turn left and go up the ridge there and you can't miss it."

The young man said, "Thank you." Then he raised the window up.

That fellow was kind of interested in the car so he reached over and pecked on the window and he lowered it again. The old man said, "What line of work are you in?"

Not knowing what else to say, the young man replied, "Well, I'm with the War on Poverty."

That fellow stepped back and looked at that car one more time and he said, "Well, it looks like you won!"

Loyal Jones

Surprise

Over here in Rockcastle County, Kentucky—they tell it for the truth—there was a fellow named Walter Blevins. He was too busy to buy clothes, and anyhow he was pretty close with his money. His wife was constantly after him to get some better clothes. Walter would raise a lot of garden stuff and take it to town and sell it. One day he got up bright and early to go to Lancaster to sell vegetables on the town square there. He had just a banner of a day, sold pert near everything he had. When he started home he pulled his mule up before a department store and said, "Whoa, Jack, I think I'll surprise Maggie tonight."

He went in and bought himself a completely new outfit: new overalls, new socks, shoes, new straw hat, got everything new, had it boxed up, put it into the back of the wagon, and headed home. It was getting about nightfall when he got to the county-line bridge over a creek. Walter stopped his mule and got down, walked around the side of the bridge where the water was swift and started taking off his clothes. He took his overalls off and threw them in the water, took off his shirt and threw it in, socks, shoes, hat, underwear—everything—and was standing there without a stitch on, said, "Yep, I'm really going to surprise Maggie tonight."

Then he walked to the back of his wagon to get his new clothes, but they had fallen off somewhere between Lancaster and the creek. Walter stood there and looked in the wagon and then down into the creek for a long time, and then he got back up on the seat of the wagon and said, "Go on, Jack, durned if we won't surprise her anyway."

> Byron Crawford
> Bagdad, Ky.
> (As told by Ky. State Rep. Danny Ford)

Family

These two men were walking down the road when they passed by a little boy leaning on his mailbox crying his eyes out. When they stopped to ask him what was wrong they heard an awful commotion back in the house, screaming and cussing and things hitting the wall. They asked him why he was crying.

"Because Mama and Daddy are up there fighting."

Since they had never seen the boy before they asked, "Whose boy are you?"

The boy paused and answered, "Well, that's what they're fightin' about."

> Bascom Lamar Lunsford
> South Turkey Creek, N.C.

Working for the Post Office

I got a real perspective on my job once when we ran short of mail carriers. I was a clerk but I had to help deliver the mail, so I get me a bag and lit out ... didn't have a uniform, a cap or badge, but I tried to dress nice.

Well, this little preschooler watched me for three or four days, and about the fourth day he came down to the mailbox, and he said, "Are you all the mailman we got?"

Another time the postmaster took me with him to visit some of the post offices he was responsible for, about ninety of them in western North Carolina. One of them was in Acorn, North Carolina, and, no kidding, it was so small that one customer and the postmaster was all that could get in there! We went in and I said to the lady postmaster, "I never have seen a post office this small. Where do you go to the bathroom?"

She said, "I go home."

"How far is that?"

"Four miles," she said.

The postmaster said, "I'm not having that." He turned to the finance man with us and said, "I want a port-a-john out here tomorrow, and I want a nice one, too, no foolishness about it!" The finance man was not taking any chances. He had a brand-new, nice two-holer sent out there.

A few days later I went with the postmaster back out there to check on it. Boy, was it a beaut! It was gleaming white. But when we looked into the post office, there wasn't anyone there.

They had moved out of the post office and into the port-a-john!

Joe Bly
Asheville, N.C.

I.Q. and Common Sense

A young man wanted a job on the railroad. He went to the personnel office, where they gave him a written examination. Afterwards they interviewed him, intending to ask him some practical questions to test his intelligence and initiative. The first question was, "Suppose you were the switchman and you heard that a freight train was coming north at sixty miles an hour and a passenger train was going south on the same track at eighty miles an hour. What would you do?"

"I'd run and get my brother."

"Why would you do that?"

"Brother ain't never seen a train wreck."

> Hon. Brooks Hays
> Little Rock, Ark.
> U.S. Representative 1942–58

The following six stories are from Albert Stewart, poet, teacher, craftsman, and founder-editor of *Appalachian Heritage,* who resides at his "Kingdom of Yellow Mountain" in Knott County, Kentucky. These stories were told by his friends and neighbors over the years.

Dilemma

A small mountain town had but two hotels. A traveler rode up, paused, and looked inquiringly about.

Traveler: "Say, which of these hotels is better?"

Town dweller: "Stranger, no matter which one you go to, you'll wish you had gone to the other."

(As told by Josiah Combs)

Working in Arkansas

One time I's out in Arkansas working fer a ole farmer out there. Pretty hard times. Come a weekend an' the ole farmer (he knowed I liked a little dram), he says, "I guess you need a little pay. I hain't got no money, but I'll see to it that you get what you want." He give me a big punkin and said, "Take that down there to the store and they'll give you credit for it." So I tuck that punkin down there and the man weighed hit and ast me what I wanted. I told him a pint of whiskey. He give me the whiskey, and I started out of there. He called out, "Hey, you forgot your change." I went back and he give me two cucumbers.

Hillbilly Repartee

One time a man in Ohio took a notion to have some fun out'n a hillbilly that was workin' with him. So he started off like this: "Got a lot of crazy people down in them hills, don't you?"

"Yep."

"Have a lot of trouble with them, don't you?"

"Nope."

"What do you do with them?"

"Send 'em to Ohio to teach school."

Layin' A-Holt of Things

One time we was workin' on a oil-drilling rig. Had that hole down maybe a half a mile, maybe more, and along come a big storm and blowed that oil well hole plumb outa the ground. Man says, "Whata we do now?"

I said, "Just hold on to your tater, and I'll let you know." Know what we done? We set to and cut that hole up into fenceposts and fenced ten acres of corn ground. Best crop you might nigh ever seen.

Old Squirrel

"One time I was out a-huntin', and I come around a swag into a kind of little open space under a big shagbark hickory and I seen this squirrel. I raised my gun to shoot it, and then I took thought and said to myself, 'Why, no, I can't kill that squirrel. He's too old. I'll just let the old feller alone. He's the oldest squirrel I ever seen. He must a been a hunnerd years old.' "

"How'd you know he was so old?"

"He was a-settin' there crackin' hickory nuts with a rock, Buddy."

Tough Groundhog

Well, another time we caught a groundhog, skinned him out, cut 'im up, and put 'im in the pot to cook. Well, we cooked that doggone thang all day and couldn't do nothing with 'im. So we cooked 'im all night and the next day he was still so tough you couldn't stick a fork in the gravy. Some fellers come along and said if we'd put bricks in and cook 'em with 'im, he'd get tender. So we put in the bricks and cooked all day. That night we took out the groundhog and throwed him away and eat the bricks.

Longer Stories

Man alone suffers so excruciatingly in the world that he was compelled to invent humor.

—FRIEDRICH NIETZSCHE

My Monkey's Your Monkey

Being a coon hunter, I hear a lot of stories about hunting. One story is about two guys that hunted together all the time and they both had a pair of dogs apiece—everybody owned their own dogs. They hunted for several years together and were buddies, huntin' buddies.

So one of these fellows took a vacation, had some relatives or something out in the West. I don't know where—out in California or Texas, Washington, somewhere way out West. And he was gone about a month. Well, his buddy was wanting to hunt, you know, and he didn't have no huntin' buddy. Naturally, soon as his buddy come back off of his vacation he run straight over to his farm and said, "When we going hunting?"

He said, "Well, we'll go tomorrow night, if you want to. Come on over."

The next night, he went over and his buddy got his dogs

and put 'em on the chain and he also got a monkey. And the guy said, "What are you doing with that monkey?"

He said, "Well, while I was on my vacation I got this monkey." Said, "You know how hard it's been, all these years we been hunting. When we tree them coons, a lot of times we can't find 'em. They're hiding up in them trees. We don't have any real good lights and sometimes there's leaves on the trees, or they're hiding up on top of them big limbs, and we just can't see 'em. You know how hard it's been to find the coons." Said, "Now, this monkey is trained for that purpose."

"Well, how does he work?"

He said, "I can't tell you, I just have to show you." So naturally his buddy was real interested in the monkey.

They went over in a big deep holler where they normally hunted and they unsnapped them dogs and turned 'em loose. The dogs went down over there and in just a little while you could hear 'em bawling. So the guy went down there leading that monkey. His buddy went right behind him, wanted to see what happened. So when he got down to the tree, there his dog was, standing with his feet up on that tree just bawling. He reached in his pocket and he got a .22 pistol out. And he handed it to that monkey. He unsnapped the monkey from his leash, and the monkey took the pistol and went up the tree. He was just up there a little bit—according to the way the story went—when *bang! bang!* Two shots, two big coons rolled out of that tree!

His friend said, "Buddy, that is really something. That's the best I ever seen." The man snapped that monkey back on his leash, put the gun back in his pocket, got the dogs, and they went on back home happy about them coons.

Couple nights later, the first guy is really wanting to go hunting again. He went over and said, "Let's go hunting again."

His friend said, "I can't." Said, "I've got an appointment. I have to go somewhere. But," he said, "you can go." Said, "You got your own dogs. Go on."

The other man said, "How 'bout me using your monkey?"

He said, "Well, there's the monkey, take it and go on. You know we're friends. My monkey's your monkey."

So the man took the monkey and he went over in the same holler where they'd killed a couple of coons the other night. He turned his dogs loose. They went down the holler there, in a little bit you could hear 'em bawling. Said, "Oh, boy. Just like the last time. Listen to them hounds. We got two coons, just like the last time." In a little bit, them dogs treed. He run down there leading that monkey fast as he could go. Sure enough, there was the big tree, just like the last time.

So immediately he took that pistol out of his pocket, handed it to the monkey, and turned that monkey loose fast. That monkey went up there and he was gone and gone. The monkey stayed up that tree and stayed up that tree and the man didn't think he was ever going to come back down. Directly, that monkey come back down the tree running as fast down it as did when he went up it. He got down to within about five foot of the ground and *bang! bang!* shot two shots, shot both that man's dogs right between the eyes!

The man said, "What happened here? This monkey went crazy. The other time he went up there and killed two coons. He went up there and stayed and stayed and now he's come back down and shot my dogs." He took and leashed that monkey back on the leash and took him back to his buddy and said, "What happened here? This monkey, he didn't do right." Said, "He went up a tree and stayed and stayed and then he come down and shot my dogs. What happened?"

His friend said, "There's something I forgot to tell you. If there's one thing that monkey hates worse than a coon, it's lying dogs."

Bill Jeffries

The Snakebit Hoe Handle

I remember a story that my uncle told about up in Summers County where he was born on my grandfather's farm. It was a steep mountain, real steep, wasn't like bottomland, it was steep hillside. There was a lot of snakes in that country, and a lot of poisonous snakes. Rattlesnakes, copperheads, real poisonous.

He said that they cleaned up this new ground and decided to plant it in corn. A real rocky, snaky place. There wasn't much soil there, you know, so they'd lay the corn down on a big flat rock and cover it up with a bunch of little rocks and what dirt they could get, to make it grow. He said the corn come up and got up about knee-high and you had to hoe it out. You couldn't plow it, it was too steep and rocky. Couldn't plow it with mules or anything.

He was up there with a hoe, hoeing that corn. And he said he was hoeing about half a day when a snake, a big copperhead, run out from under one of them rocks and bit his hoe handle. He said his hoe handle started swelling up, said it swelled up into a big log. He said he went down to his woodshed and got a crosscut saw or a one-man saw, whichever it was he was using—I believe he said a crosscut saw—took one handle off of it. Sawed that hoe handle up into logs. Went down to the barn and got a team of oxens out of the barn and went up there and put a chain on them logs, drug 'em down to a sawmill and had 'em sawed up in lumber. Said they took that lumber and built him a house. There was some lumber left over after he got his house built, so he sold it and took the money and went on a vacation. Said when he come back, the swelling had went out of his house and choked his cat to death.

Bill Jeffries

Editors' Note: In Richard Chase's book, *American Folk Tales and Songs* (Dover, 1985), this story ends: "... Built me a new chickenhouse. Then I painted it, and don't you know!—the turpentine in the paint took out all that swellin', and the next morning my chickenhouse had shrunk to the size of a shoe box. Good thing I hadn't put my chickens in it!"

You Can't Please Everybody

There was an old man and his grandson had a mule and the mule's name was Hiney. They're taking him to sell him at the marketplace. So they take their mule named Hiney and they're walking along and there's these two old men playing checkers up on the side, on the porch there. One of them says, "Well, isn't that about the dumbest thing you ever seen in your life? There is a strong mule being led by two men, one of them could at least get up on it and save himself some trouble." Well, they didn't want to be thought of as stupid so the grandfather gets up on top of Hiney.

They're walking along and pass the church, and the women's meeting was just breaking up. One of them comes out there and sees the old grandfather and she says, "My, my! There is a man who is making his poor grandson walk on the ground beside of him. He's lived a long life, he ought to be able to walk himself." So he gets off the mule and has his grandson get up there.

They're walking by the bridge. A man comes by and says, "That's one of the most disgraceful things I've ever seen in my life. There's a grandson making his poor old grandfather walk beside of him. He could just as easily get down and show some respect for his elders." So they both get up there. They pass the veterinarian's office and he says, "Now, look at that. They're making that poor old beast of burden suffer, both of them people riding on top of him. That's disgraceful." So both of them get down, and hoist Hiney up on their shoulders—they should have known they was in trouble when they got their Hiney up past their shoulders.

Anyway, they walk along the gorge and there's crowds of people laughing at seeing that mule trying to get off the two folks. The mule gets so doggone scared that he jumps right down the thousand-foot drop into the gorge where he was killed dead.

Now, there's a moral to that story. You try to please everybody and you wind up losing your Hiney.

Eric Waggoner

Uncle Ketchup and Aunt Tomato

I'll tell you about my Uncle Ketchup. He lived in Selma, Alabama. That's where all my people come from. They come up here to shake the money tree in the coal mines and make a lot of money. So when I was ten years old they took me back to see my Uncle Ketchup. He had a farm there, and that farm was kind of rough. He got it in Reconstruction days, forty acres and a mule. Twenty acres of it was poor and twenty acres was rich. Now, that poor side, you couldn't raise a fuss on that. But on that rich side you could throw a grain of corn in a place, and before you could cover it up it was about two foot high. It was *growing*.

I'll tell you what happened one morning. My Aunt Tomato, my Uncle Ketchup's wife, got up one morning about five o'clock and she came out, washing and humming on that washboard. She hung up her clothes and she went back and got some more and she come back. When she got back she couldn't find the others. See, this was that *rich* land. When she came out that last time them first clothes she hung up had gone about three miles down the road. She'd missed the clothesline and hung them on a pumpkin vine!

Don't you know they had to put roller skates on the big pumpkins to keep them from dragging the little pumpkins to death?

Nat Reese
Princeton, W.Va.

Answered Prayer

This story is about a man in Chattanooga who had a cat. Every time they went on vacation, they had to take the cat down to the "cattery" and board it for a couple of weeks until they got back. The cat got wise after so long; he didn't like to go stay in that place; he wanted to stay home. Out back, behind the house, was a row of Lombardy poplars—if you know what these trees are. They are just about ten inches around and two hundred feet tall—the tallest, thinnest trees you've seen in your life. Well, that cat figured out if he went far enough up in that tree, there was no way that man could get to him. So, the next time the man started to go on vacation with his wife, he went out back to get the cat and the cat saw him coming and went straight up that tree and got out of reach!

The man said, "We can't go on vacation until we get the cat down."

She said, "How in the world are we going to get it down?"

He said to get the rope in the barn and she did. He climbed as far as he could up in that tree and tied the rope around the tree trunk and came back down and tied it to the rear bumper of the car.

He said, "I'm going to pull this tree ahead and when it gets low enough, you reach up and get the cat and we'll take it to the cattery."

She said, "Okay."

So he pulled the car up and he looked through the rearview mirror and saw the tree coming down toward him, so he stopped.

His wife said, "Pull up a little farther, honey, I can't reach the cat yet!"

So, he pulled up about two more feet, and he saw the tree come down farther so he stopped.

She yelled, "I still can't reach him yet, just about two more feet, honey!"

So he was pulling it the last two feet and looked back and saw the rope begin to fray. And before she could reach and get the cat, the rope broke! Well, the last they saw of that cat, he was going over that row of Lombardy poplars, and when he went out of sight, he was still going up! They said, later, that that cat went over the row of trees, went over a shopping center and five city blocks!

Well, the man and his wife decided they wouldn't go on vacation because they felt so bad about the cat, so they spent the next two days looking for the cat. Couldn't find it anywhere! The wife went to the store, and she ran into a friend of hers who lived five or six blocks down the street and this friend was buying cat food.

She said, "I didn't know you had a cat."

The friend said, "We didn't, but you know we'd been wanting one and, night before last, Clarence and I were sitting in the back yard charcoaling and all of a sudden, this cat came flying down out of the air and landed on our patio.

"Clarence looked over at me and said, 'Ethel, the good Lord has sent us a cat.' "

> *Bob Terrell*
> *Asheville, N.C.*

Three Drinking Buddies

There was these three drunks, we'll say they was drinking buddies, and one of them died. He was down at the funeral home. The day before he was supposed to be buried, the two of them got together and went to see him. They stood looking at him, one of them said, "Boy, don't he look natural. It looks just like him!"

The other one said, "Well, it ought to, it's *him*, ain't it?"

As they stood there with a tear in their eye, one said, "By golly, just for old times' sake, we ought to have another drink with him. Let's just pick up old Joe and take him around to the corner bar." There wasn't anybody around, so they picked up old Joe and took him to the bar, took him back in this dark corner, propped him up on the barstool . . . fixed his arm, you know, so he wouldn't fall.

They sat there and drank several toasts, talked about the good times, till one of them got hot and said, "Boy, it's kinda close in here. I think I'll step outside for a breath of air."

The other one said, "Well, you ain't leaving me in here by myself with old Joe! I'm coming too."

So they stepped outside. Soon as they left, the bartender came over and took one look at old Joe sitting there, said, "My goodness, buddy, you look like the dickens. You've had enough. Let's go!"

Well, he didn't move . . . didn't say a word, you know . . . him being dead that-a-way. So the bartender says again, "Okay, bud, you've had enough, now, so let's go outside. Come on!" And he jiggled old Joe's arm, which unpropped him, and he fell off the stool onto the barroom floor.

The bartender got kind of alarmed at that, so he kneeled down and tried to rouse old Joe, and put his ear down to listen to his heart.

About that time, the two drinking buddies came back in, said, "Hey, hold on here! Bartender, what are you doing? Have you killed our buddy?"

The bartender jumped up off the floor and said without hesitation, "The son-of-a-gun drew a knife on me!"

Aunt Jenny Wilson
Peach Creek, W.Va.

Tucker's Knob and the Weather

I really am from Tucker's Knob, just a little ole wide place in the road. But it's a pretty little old town . . . The moon comes over the mountain in gallon fruit jars!

It's so small, we don't have a town drunk. We just take turns!

In 1937 it got down to 165 below zero. It was so cold if you went outside all you could hear was total silence. If anyone said anything all you could do was grab a handful of words and sentences and take 'em in by the fire, to tell what they said.

I went out to milk the cow and, boy, was she cold! I took my warm hands out of my pockets, put 'em on that cow . . . she turned around and said, "Thank ye, thank ye!"

It was so cold I saw a couple of beagle dogs putting a

set of jumper cables on a rabbit, trying to get it started!

But you talk about obtuse weather . . . it started fairing up after that, and 1938 turned out to be the hottest and driest it had ever been. It didn't rain from February to Septober. Hot, dry and droughty. One fellow got out there and started praying, "Oh, Lord, let it rain, please let it rain . . . not for me, I'd just like for my two boys to see it!"

It got so dry, people at the Baptist Church started sprinkling and the Methodists just used a damp cloth.

Didn't rain but one drop of water all summer. John Malt had walked out and looked up at the sky . . . that one drop hit him right between the eyes. He fainted. Had to pour two buckets of dust on him to revive him!

We lost a good team of mules because of that hot weather. We didn't raise nothing but a little crop of popcorn. Me and Daddy hitched the wagon to the mules and went down there to pick those little ears of popcorn. We picked and it got hotter and hotter. We had about a half a wagon-load full, when I got so hot and Papa got so hot and those mules got so hot and that popcorn got so hot . . . well, it started popping. It was flying everywhere, out of the field, out of the wagon, and when those mules saw all that popcorn they thought it was snow. They froze to death! Right there in the middle of July!

It was so hot and dry we had an awful time trying to find fish bait. All the red worms, grub worms, honeybees and waspers, all the insects and critters had gone a mile down in the ground looking for water. You just can't find fish bait in that kind of weather.

But I was walking down the road and lying on the side of the road there, there was a black snake. He'd swallowed a frog and just the hind legs of that frog were sticking out of that old snake's mouth. I looked at that snake and he looked at me, and I said to myself, "Myself, if I had that frog I bet I could catch me a big fish down at the mill pond."

I picked up that black snake and tried to pull that frog out of his mouth, but he wouldn't let go. Then I remembered the snakebite medicine I had in my hip pocket. So I took out that cough syrup bottle and poured about two tablespoons full of that 100-proof moonshine down that snake's throat. Boy, he just grinned when he tasted that liquid fire, and when he opened his mouth wider I yanked that frog out of his mouth.

When I got to the mill pond, I hooked that frog on my fishing pole and threw him out in the water. He'd no sooner hit the water, I don't reckon, until I heard a racket behind me and felt something nudge me. I turned around and looked, and there was that same old black snake with another frog in his mouth!

And that's the truth!

Ernest "Doc" McConnell
Rogersville, Tenn.

The Mule Egg

Old Steamer liked livestock, especially mules, and he lived and breathed until the day that he could, finally, have a mule of his own! Boy, he loved mules! Every time anybody had a team of mules and went up the road, he'd go out to the fence and watch them go by.

He's always asking people, "You don't know anybody that's got a litter of mules so I could git me a little baby mule, do ye? Boy, I'd love to have me a baby mule—I'd like to have a nice little brown, hairy, fluffy, long-eared baby mule—just a little ole mule I could have for my own and I could raise it up and it'd git just about that big; and I could put my little toy harness on it, and hook it to my little toy plow and I could plow with that; boy, I'd love to have me a little baby mule that I could raise up as my own!"

And he lived and breathed that some day he'd have him a nice little brown, fluffy, long-eared baby mule that he could raise up as his own, and he aggravated everybody in the community to death, wanting him a baby mule; asked everybody! Wanted Momma and Daddy to put one in his sock at Christmastime, you know! Couldn't wait until, some day, he could have him a baby mule!

One day he walked into the country store, where all the men were sitting around that pot-bellied stove, laughing and giggling, drinking yellow dopes and eating Moon Pies. They were on about their third yellow dope and fourth Moon Pie, when old Steamer come in—and they wuz looking for something to talk about. Old John, at the country store, had just got in a shipment of them big old round coconuts, about that big! You've seen them big old round, hairy things about that big? A whole basket full of them sitting over there and old Steamer kept eyeballing them things and looked at them men sittin' round the stove.

Finally, he got up enough courage and nerve and asked, "What's them old brown, hairy, round things laying over there?"

John said, "Well, Steamer, don't you know what them things is?"

He said, "No, what is them things?"

John said, "Why, them things is mule eggs. Every one of them has a baby mule in it and if you take that home and set on it for about two weeks, you'll hatch you out a little baby mule!"

"Hot doggie, I've always wanted me a baby mule!" Steamer said. "You mean there's baby mules in there?"

He said, "Yeah, them's mule eggs. That's where little baby mules come from. Git you one of them and set on it for two weeks and keep it good and warm, and you'll hatch you out a little baby mule!"

Well, old Steamer worked him out 35 cents and got him one of them old brown, round, hairy coconuts and carried that mule egg home like some family jewel. Carried it all the way to the house and got him an old split basket and put it out there by the woodshed and put him some straw and hay in it and put that old mule egg in the middle of it and climbed up on that old coconut and started counting them days, you know. Momma let him bring it in the house at night and put it under the bed covers and brung his meals out there to him during the day. And old Steamer started counting the days—one, two, three, four, five . . . he knowed just any day now that mule egg was going to pop

open and there was going to be him a nice little brown,
fluffy, long-eared baby mule—just what he always
wanted, you know!

He started countin' them days off—seven, eight, nine,
ten, eleven, twelve—couldn't wait until that mule egg
opened right up and there was going to be him a little baby
mule! Thirteen—fourteen—fifteen—sixteen—seventeen
days come and went and that mule egg never did hatch out,
and he finally decided it must be a bad egg and took it out
there behind the woodshed, held it up to the light and
looked at it, smelled it, and even held it up to his ear to see
if he could hear a little baby mule a-kickin' in there or
anything, you know, and decided it must be a bad egg! He
took that old brown, hairy coconut down behind the
woodshed—in disgust and aggravation—and heaved that
old mule egg down into the briar patch!

Well, it hit right in the middle of a briar patch and sitting in the briar patch was an old flop-eared rabbit. And,
about the time that old coconut hit the briar patch, that old
rabbit got scared and jumped out of the briar patch and run
off across the cabbage field there, and old Steamer seen
that rabbit and thought it was a little baby mule, and he
chased it all evening, a-hollering, "Come back here, come
back here, I'm your mammy, I'm your mammy!"

Then he said, "Aw, go to hell. I wouldn't be able to
plow that fast, nohow!"

Ernest "Doc" McConnell
Rogersville, Tenn.

Something Out of Place

With his crow-black hair parted in the middle, and his
long-sleeved shirt buttoned at the collar, Herbert stands a
good foot taller than Miss Merit, our third-grade teacher.
He doesn't belong in the picture. He didn't belong in the
third grade. Back then, in the early 1940s, he seemed to
me less a classmate than one of the old people I saw in oval
picture frames on dimly-lit parlor walls.

Old-fashioned, quiet, solemn, Herbert walked among

us, slow-moving, deliberate, like a farmer in waist-high weeds. The only time I ever saw him in a playful mood was when he'd take a bucket lid and go about the playground pretending he was driving a car. Even then he drove slowly, like my grandfather, gave his signals, and backed up carefully. Herbert loved cars, and although his family had no car—only a team and wagon—he knew all the makes and models.

I guess Herbert had been held back several times. He turned sixteen in the third grade and stopped coming to school. Once or twice after that I saw him driving his daddy's wagon and team. I forgot about Herbert until— several years later—a movie was made in our community.

The movie was *Tap Roots*. It had a Civil War setting and moviemakers needed people with horses and wagons. I think they offered $25 a day for a driver, wagon and team. Lots of people showed up at Snelson's dairy barn—among them Herbert, with his daddy's team and wagon.

The moviemakers worked all morning getting the wagons lined up. They were going to film the wagons hurrying through a nearby gap, as if in retreat from some battle. There were delays. When it looked like everything was ready, something would happen to hold up the filming. Lunchtime came. Everybody ate box lunches—off wagon beds, and at tables set up in front of the dairy barn.

After lunch there were more delays. Finally, everything was ready. People ran shouting up and down the line of wagons. The wagons started moving—slowly, then faster and faster. The cameras were filming it all. There was Herbert, driving the last wagon to go through the gap.

As Herbert's wagon passed out of sight, somebody ran over and said something to the director, who started hollering and cursing. He stomped, hollered, kicked, and cursed. A little crowd gathered around him and walked in circles with him while he kept hollering and kicking the ground and cursing. For a long time we didn't know what was wrong. Then we understood it was some trouble with Herbert's wagon. They had him come back. The moviemakers hadn't noticed—and those of us watching hadn't, either—

that Herbert, the last driver through the gap, had an old 1947 North Carolina automobile license plate tacked on the back of his daddy's wagon.

Dr. Jim Wayne Miller
Bowling Green, Ky.

Impounded

Way it started, Wiley Wolford and Junior Crumm started out to Columbus, Ohio, to get work—about the forty-eleventh time they'd been up there. But they never lasted long, always ended up right back down here. Wiley and Junior started out in a pretty good old car—'71 Chevrolet. Looked rough but run good. And $300 between them.

Boys, it's not but about 150 miles from here to Columbus, but by the time they got there they didn't have any money left but a little change. And run out of gas. What they'd done was stop at every beer joint between here and there. They couldn't remember, actually, what happened to their money.

Anyways, there they were, out of gas on High Street in Columbus. Junior he knowed you could go down to the welfare and they'd give you a voucher for gas if you was stranded. My opinion, when they taken a look at Junior and Wiley, they'd give them all the gas it took just to get them out of the state. They had to wait there in a big room amongst these old shaky people and sick people and people talking to themselves and people that would get up and run around the room acting like they were driving a car, making the noise of the motor—*uuuuuhd-un, uuuuuhd-un!* Junior said he never seen anything like it in his life, it made him uneasy being around people like that. Till finally it come their turn and they told what happened to them. Run out of money and then out of gas, looking for work and all. And they got the voucher for gas. Well, they got the gas in a can—Wiley had to leave his billfold at the station before they'd let them take the can—and poured it in the tank and went to start back up. Car wouldn't start. Raised the hood, son-of-a-gun, somebody'd stole the battery. Fairly new battery, too, Junior said.

Wasn't nothin to do but go back to the welfare—it was right close by—and they did, and set there in the waiting room with all the crazy people till it come their turn again, and told the woman what had happened to them—and got a voucher for a battery. Junior and Wiley says the welfare in Ohio is real good to you.

They went and got a battery. They'd been in the welfare all that time and had left their car there with the hood up, and when they got back to it, why, it wasn't there. Gone. Well, that floored 'em.

They'd been so lucky with the welfare so far, they went right back. Said the woman couldn't believe it when they got to see her again, the third time that day. It was right at closing time by then. Told her this time somebody stole the whole car.

The welfare lady said it wasn't stolen, probably, said the police had probably towed it off—impounded it. She got on the telephone and called around and, sure enough, found out it had been towed off by the police and was out at a place where they impounded cars that looked like they'd just been left on the street. But there'd be a charge to get it out and, anyway, they couldn't get it now till the next day. So this welfare lady give Wiley and Junior another voucher for room and board for the night and next morning, told 'em where to go, and all. She even arranged to have 'em come back the next morning and she'd have 'em a paper to get their car with, and even have somebody drive 'em out to where their car was. Junior and Wiley says the welfare in Ohio is real good to you. If you get stranded like they was the welfare'll really take care of you.

Well, they done just what they's supposed to. Got down to the welfare next morning, got a ride out there to pick up their car, got there, got to checkin' on it, and found it. There'd been a mess-up in the paperwork, though, was how they explained it, and their car was already crushed. Compacted. Junior said they did locate it, only it wasn't no bigger than a bale of hay. Still, they could recognize it, because they'd compacted it with their clothes still in it,

and they could see part of one of their shirts stickin' out.

The welfare couldn't do anything about that, now. It was just a mistake, such as anybody could make. But they did give Wiley and Junior bus tickets back home. Junior said he wasn't mad at anybody, it was just one of those things that happens, and the welfare there in Columbus was just as nice as could be. But Junior and Wiley's not been to Columbus to look for work lately—nor anywheres.

Dr. Jim Wayne Miller
Bowling Green, Ky.

The Bet, or Two Foolish Husbands

Once upon a time, back when turkeys chewed tobacco, there were two women, Regina Mae and Willameana. These two women were the best of friends but whenever they got together they always started arguing . . . arguing about who could stitch the prettiest quilts, who could spit the farthest, whose chickens laid the biggest eggs . . . that sort of thing.

One day they got to talking about their husbands and how foolish they could act. They started bickering, fussing and arguing until they decided to make a bet as to which one could make the biggest fool out of her husband. They gave each other a week to do it in.

Now, Willameana knew her husband *so* well. You see, he always thought he was sick, and getting sicker. If someone complained of a headache, within seconds he'd say, "I think I have a headache too!" Or if someone started scratching with poison ivy, pretty soon he'd just start making music on his arm . . . that sort of thing. So when her old man came through the front door, she asked him, "Honey, do you feel all right?"

"I think I'm just fine," he said, "but I'm open to suggestions."

She said, "You are looking right puny. Come over here and sit down, and I'm going to fix you up as best I can." She went over to the fireboard, got her down some medicine and dosed him with it. Then she kinda worried over him, gave him mush for supper and sent him off to bed real early. And there he was, you know, just laying in that bed with a little half-smile on his face. He felt pretty good but he knew Willameana thought he was getting sick.

Next morning she shook him awake and said, "Stick out your tongue! Oh," she said, "I hope you're not going to put that thing back into your mouth! From the looks of it you've come down with something, but I'm going to take care of you the best I can." And she went out to the herb garden and got some angelica and spigmint to thicken and thin his blood. And she kind of fretted over him all day and into the night, and by then his little smirk had turned upside down into a frown. He was real concerned that maybe he couldn't lift his head off the pillow!

Meanwhile, back at Regina Mae's house . . . now, she had a different tactic for winning that bet.

When her husband came through the door she was sitting behind her loom, throwing the shuttle back and forth —*click-wham, click-wham!* And it without a single piece of thread on it! Well, her husband looked, and watched and looked, and finally he said, "Regina Mae, what is it that you're doing?"

And she said, "Why, I'm weaving." And before he had a chance to say another word, she came back with, "Oh, this is the *finest* thread that I've ever worked with. Folks that sold it to me said it has a special quality ... said it comes from virgin sheep and any husband lying to his wife, why, he can't even see it at all!"

Well, he peered down closer, took off his specs and cleaned them some, said, "You know, I believe that might be some of the finest thread that I've ever laid eyes on!"

Regina Mae just smiled real big and for the next two or three days, whenever her husband came through the door, there she sat behind the loom throwing the shuttle back and forth in mid-air.

Meanwhile, back at Willameana's, she had done a good job of convincing her husband that he was just about ready to take his last dying breath. She said, "Honey, I'm sure gonna miss you when you're gone." She sort of cried along, said, "I just hate to tell you this, but I've done had your coffin made. And while you've got enough strength left in you, you sure could help me a powerful lot if you'd just help me get you into it!"

She brought that coffin and paralleled it to the bed and said, "It makes me sad to ask you to move yourself from your deathbed into your coffin," and she cried and carried on.

He said, "Willameana, I've thought of something sadder than that. When a friend dies, you lose a friend. But when *you* die, you lose *all* your friends!" They kept crying and she just kind of flipped and flopped him a couple of real good turns and landed him right into that coffin. She thought it was a good sign, 'cause he landed *face up*.

She just petted him there on the belly and by the time he closed those hypochondriac, beady eyes, darned if he didn't look beyond peaceful.

Meanwhile, back at Regina Mae's house, next time her husband came in, she said, "Honey, would you help me move this-here bolt of cloth over to that table? Watch out, and don't let it drag the floor!" They got over the table and she acted like she was spreading out the material, got her scissors and went to cutting.

He watched and looked and finally he said, "Regina Mae, what is it you're making?"

She said, "Why, I'm making you the finest suit of clothes you'll ever put on!" And she kept cutting, and went to sewing, stitching that needle in and out of thin air! Her husband went on to bed.

Next morning she said, "Honey, it's ready for you to try on!" He came into the parlor and she held it up, so he figured that must be the trousers, so he put one leg in and then the other. "Raise your arms up," she said, and she slipped something on his arms, so he figured that must be the shirt. She held up one more time and he figured that must be the jacket. So he kinda backed right into it.

"Would you look at that!" she said. "Turn around. There!" He turned around twice and she said, "You know, I think it's a perfect fit!" And him standing there in nothing but a pair of boots!

That same morning at Willameana's, she just leaned off the side of the bed and said in a loud voice toward the coffin, "Law me, he's done died during the night!" And her old man figured she must be right. So she got busy and spread the word throughout the entire community that she wanted everybody to go down to the burial ground for what could turn out to be a *revival* of sorts.

Then she got a neighbor to help her load up that big old heavy, wooden coffin box full of her husband onto the wagon, and . . . "Gee-haw!" She started off down the road to the cemetery.

When she got there folks were clustered all around. And who should be coming down the road but Regina Mae and her old man . . . and him in his new suit of clothes!

He was walking along shaking hands with every other one and telling them all about his fine new suit of clothes and . . . well, folks didn't quite know what to do! They just stared at first. Then a few of the children started giggling. Then the preacher threw back his head and howled. Then everyone started in laughing, slapping their legs and making so much ruckus that the dead man got curious. He sat up in his coffin to see what was going on!

Folks ran in all directions. Then the dead man got a glimpse of his neighbor in his *new suit*, and he started laughing too. He laughed so hard he almost fell out of the coffin. Then it dawned on folks that there was some foolishness going on, so they all came back to find out what-and-all was happening.

Of course, they found out that Regina Mae and Willameana had done gone and made a bet as to which one was married to the biggest fool . . . both of whom were now on display!

Folks may have decided which one won the bet, but Regina Mae and Willameana never did settle it. Why, to this day you can walk into that community and find them still bickering, arguing, fussing, yelling back and forth. Law, they sound *downright foolish!*

> *Connie Regan and Barbara Freeman*
> *Asheville, N.C.*

Barbara Freeman and Connie Regan-Black have traveled the world as "The Folktellers" and are pioneers in the storytelling renaissance. You can hear them tell "The Bet, or Two Foolish Husbands" on their fourth album, *Friends*, MTA#2. For information on *Friends* as well as the other award-winning Folkteller recordings—*White Horses and Whippoorwills*, MTA#1, *Chillers*, MTA#2, and *Tales to Grow On*, Weston Woods, contact: Mama T-Artists/Folktellers, P. O. Box 1920, Dept. B, Asheville, NC 28802, (704) 258-1113.

Rescued

I want to tell you a story about the first motorcycle in Black Mountain, North Carolina. You see, folks in Black Mountain, right down the road from where I lived, had heard of a motorcycle after World War II, but nobody in the whole town had seen one.

So that day when ole Leroy Teets came in from the

Navy with this brand new blue and chrome Harley-David-son motorcycle, folks came out of their stores and out of their homes to see what was making all of that racket! Well, that thing was a sight to behold . . . They said it had a headlight as big as a dinner plate! The seat was as wide as a buckboard; had a big ole ruby-studded mudflap right in the very back. Had a windshield that came almost as high as his head, and some folks said that thing was even "air-conditioned."

Now, they could tell that Leroy was happy and they could tell he was proud—all they had to do was just to count the bugs on his teeth! Now, instead of coming up and saying how "fine" that thing was, some of those mountain boys came up and started teasing him and taunting him.

They said, "Well, what is this old thing, Leroy? Why, you can't take this thing on these old mountain roads—this is just a play-purty!"

He said, "I can take it anywhere in the county!"

One boy said, "You can't, Leroy; this thing looks like a pregnant bicycle!" They were teasing him and taunting him!

'Bout that time, old Jeeter Ledford walked up and said, "Leroy, I bet you can't take that thing where my mule can go!"

Leroy said, "I bet I can take this motorcycle anywhere your ole mule can go!"

"All right," said Jeeter, "I'll bet you $5 that you can't ride up to the top of High Windy! I have rid my mule up to the top of that mountain!"

Now, old Leroy had this habit of speaking before he thought. He pulled $5 out of his pocket and threw it on the ground, and Jeeter pulled $5 out of his pocket and threw it on the ground. Then old Leroy started up that motorcycle . . . *vroom, vroom, vroom*. Now old High Windy is a long, tall steep mountain . . . there's no road nor no trail to the top; it's just rocks, sticks, leaves and trees all the way to the top. Ole Leroy had to have it in full throttle and hold on for everything he was worth just to stay on the mountain.

What they all forgot about was old Rhubarb Golightly,

who lived away up at the top of High Windy. Now, Rhubarb was a man that didn't like people. He hadn't been to
town for seven years and didn't care if he ever went to
town again! He just lived up at the top of High Windy with
his little wife, Samantha, and he did all his own chores and
grew all his own food, and he was used to hearing the
sounds of birds, and bees, and things like that. So, that
day, after old Rhubarb Golightly had finished his big old
dinner of biscuits and sow-belly gravy, skunk cabbage,
poke sallet, jar-bean pie with possum sauce, and two
mouth-shrinking dill pickles, he went out on the front
porch and sat down out there to take his ease.

Just then he heard something coming up through there
—*vroom, vrooooom*. He jumped up; he'd never heard a
man or a bear make a sound like that...*va-room,
vroooom*. Then he saw it coming, that headlight was just
a-flashing, there were dogs a-running, sticks a-flying and
chickens going, *Quack, mauk, cluck, cluck*.

He said, "Samantha, bring me my gun!" She brings him
his big old gun and he levels that thing and goes, *Bang,
bang*, and that motorcycle goes flying that way, and ole
Leroy goes flying that way!

And she said, "Did you kill it, honey?"

He says, "I don't know, but whatever that thing was, I
shore made it turn that boy loose!"

David Holt
Fairview, N.C.

You can hear David Holt telling this story on his award-winning record *The Hairy Man and Other Wild Tales*, available
from High Windy Records, P. O. Box 553, Fairview, NC
28730.

The following two stories were submitted by George Daugh-
erty, famous storyteller and saw-player of West Virginia, who
got them from his dear friend, Sam Chilton, another great
storyteller, before Sam died in 1977. They are told by Riley

Wilson, regarded by both these men as West Virginia's great-est storyteller of all. They both point out that Riley was an "elocutionist," someone who could elaborate on a tale and get more laughs out of it than they could, mentioning also his richness of detail and his potent asides.

Reach Me the Tin

At the head of Hart's Creek in Lincoln County, West Virginia, lives a man named Jim Sizemore. Ninety-seven years of age, he has nineteen grown children, all of them married and propagating. Hasn't got a tooth in his head. Has long whiskers. You can take two currycombs and get six pounds of tobacco out of his beard in one whop.

I was a candidate for office down there. They asked me to go out and see old man Sizemore. I said I wouldn't ride 65 miles on a mule to see John the Baptist . . . I'd catch him court week in Hamlin, knowing he'd be in there trying to get on the jury.

I rode 35 miles on a mule all night. I got over there about eight o'clock in the morning. First man I saw at the courthouse was Jim, refereeing a horseshoe match. Just as I got up to him I heard him say in that old feeble voice of his, says, "Boys . . . hit's a leaner. Three." A boy cut notches in a stick.

I tied up my mule, I struck him on the back, I said, "Hello, Jim, how are ye?"

He looked up at me a minute or two, and said, "Hello, thar."

I said, "How ye been?"

Said, "By gum, hit's Wilson, hain't it?" Said, "I ain't no good no more." I asked him what was the matter.

"That ole farm of mine," he said, "by gosh, hit's wore plumb out. Can't scratch a living on it. Imple-mints all busted. Elmer, that's Minnie's boy, that's the onliest hand I got left on the place. Cut his heel on a scythe. Damned nigh cut his leg off. Had to get a doctor fer him. My woman she's been down with the misery all year. Wilson, it's hell fer a man to have his woman down, specially in the winter. I got a aged daughter giving me some trouble. And old Ring, that fox dog of mine, damned if he didn't die yes-tiddy."

I said, "Well, Jim, you're in pretty bad shape. Come back here and let me see you a moment." I took him back in the sheriff's office, had a gallon jug of Bellow Nelson eighteen-year-old whiskey, about 108-proof. I said, "Jim, let's take a little drink."

He said, "I ain't given to drinkin' none. But I b'lieve I will take a drop or two with you this morning." There was an old water cooler sitting over in the window shade, a tin cup sitting by it. He says, "Reach me the tin." I handed him this pint tin cup, filled it up to the brim. He held it up to his nose, said, "Four or five months old, hain't it?" And he drank that pint of whiskey.

I said to myself, by god, I've killed him! 'Cause I didn't think it was possible for a man 97 years of age for his heart to stand the shock of a pint of whiskey 108-proof. But I saw the perspiration sort of break out on his brow and I knew he could handle it. I said, "Jim, you'll get out of this trouble you're in."

This whiskey started taking ahold on him. He said, "Yes, I reckon I will. Yes, I'll get out of it. But that old farm of mine, Wilson, hit is in bad shape. I scratched around there 97 years and got my younguns raised. I guess I'll make it now. Elmer, that's Minnie's boy, he did cut his heel up pretty bad on a scythe. But he's a Sizemore, full-blooded people. He'll heal up. My woman she's been down with the misery all year, but I got a fair patent medicine for her. She'll be up there next time of court. I got a aged daughter, but that is prov-adent. Godamighty never give her to me on no purpose of His'n. He jes' drapped her an' I ketched her, that's all. And Old Ring, that fox dog of mine, now, Wilson, I am a-missin' him."

I said, "Uncle Jim, let's take another little drink."

He said, "Reach me the tin."

He poured out another pint of whiskey. Now, in five minutes he's got a quart of this old 108-proof whiskey in him, and I said to him, I said, "Uncle Jim, you're so much older than I. Your life's so much fuller than mine. Age can teach you more than I could possibly learn, but if you'll pardon me, sir, please don't think there's any presumption on my part a-tall, but I say to you life seems to me to be just a great big wheel. It's constantly turning. At the bottom of the wheel of life is birth, the top is death, and, Uncle Jim, there's always one side of the wheel in the shadow, but it turns into the sun. And that's all they is to life ... there's birth, death, sunshine and shadow. And when that wheel turns into the sun, you'll get out of this trouble."

Well, he reached back into his hip pocket and he combed off a twist of burley tobacco. He looked at me two or three minutes and he mumbled to himself, "Trouble. Yes, trouble."

He said, "Who in the hell told you I's in any trouble? I got the best damn farm there are in Lincoln. That thirty-six acres down there on the creek bottom ... sow seeds and it lights a-growing. Elmer, that's Minnie's boy, he did cut his heel up pretty bad on a scythe, but just like a squirrel he's up and running. My woman she's been down with the misery all year, but I'll bet ye a five-dollar bill, take ye off there at the place and hook her up to a singletree, she'll out-pull ary damn mule in the county. I got a aged daughter but she's Faith. And old Ring, that fox dog of mine, he was a good dog in his day, Wilson, but he was a-gittin' old. I took him out the other night for a little private chase and damned if I didn't catch him a-backtracking. And when the kill come he was back there three or four mile barkin' with the puppies. I'd had to shoot him. Ye can't keep no sich a-dog as that in your pack. You might accidentally breed to him and catch yourself a backtracker.

"Come out some time. Bring the Prosecutin' Attorney and the Sheriff. Bring all the candidates out there. We'll go up on the mountain and have a chase, come back and put the woman in the kitchen. And I'll have food, fellows, and whiskey for every damn man in the county. Wilson, reach me the tin!"

Riley Wilson

Hell in the Holler

Down on Big Ugly Creek in Lincoln County there was an old fellow lived there name of Brown. He was Justice of the Peace and he'd been Justice of the Peace till the mind of man runneth not to the contrary.

He never tried a case. He could neither read nor write. And his alibi for not trying was that he didn't want them circuit judges runnin' over his papers.

We's up there running foxes one morning, sitting on a log eating a sandwich . . . he called it a snack . . . just a yellow biscuit full of apple butter, drinking out of a fruit jar and every time he'd raise it up it'd raise a whop across his nose and I says, "Squire, take back off that crock. You're gonna tear your head off with it."

He said, "My woman said if I didn't start drinking out of a bucket I's liable to have a cancer."

I saw the old feller was going to sleep on me and I thought I'd keep him awake. I says, "Squire, how are you gettin' along with the law?"

He said, "Wilson, folks ain't livin' neighborly up here a-tall no more. They're just a-fightin' one t'other you can't put a crop in fer 'em. And right down here at the foot of this mountain where them Spurlocks and Medcalfs live . . . married in to one t'other and live like a lot of damn dogs . . . inbred. Here comes one of 'em now. Peer down the race, now, they've had another fight down there."

I looked down the ridge and here come Jim Medcalf. Had on a little clawhammer coat. A little flat joe of a derby, a celluloid collar, 'stead of having a button he had a hook. He had an Adam's apple running up and down his neck, it looked like a fishing worm had swallowed a croquet ball. So I said to him, "Good morning, Mr. Medcalf."

He said, "Well as common."

Jim said, "How are ye, Squire?"

He said, "I'm middling-like." Said, "Squire, y'all had a big chase out there, didn't ye, this morning? I heered ye dogs and I's aiming to come, but we've had hell in our holler again. I'm gonna tell it to ye if it takes me till morning and if I forget one p'int in it I'm going back and tell it over to ye again. Yesterday evening after I got my work done, I'm sittin' on a rock in front of the house. Sun was about a half an hour high. No, my god, it couldn't a-been over fifteen minutes high. I was sittin' there just a-peeking and a-peering. And I peered down the road and I seed a feller coming with a woman and a little bitty girl. Well, my eyesight ain't as pert as it used to be . . . couldn't recognize nobody at no big distance. And my wife, Octave, she peeked through a crack in the house and she said, 'By damned, if it ain't your sister Lockhoney!'

"Well, I peered down the road and I said, 'I be damned if it ain't! She married Abner Spurlock, damned one-eyed son of a . . . he fit in the Yankee Army! And moved to Californy. Californy's way out yonder somewhere ye got to git a ticket fer to git to it.

" 'Well,' I said to my woman, 'reckon they're hungry?'

"And she said, 'Reckon they air.' Well, we'd churned there that morning . . . we made 'em up some wheat bread, and they et hearty. After they got through eating we never took a time fer to clean a dish nor nothing, just pushed the table back agin the wall. And my little girl got to playing with my sister's little girl and I vow and hope to God they ain't a half a pound atwixt them. Hit's a plumb sight the way they look like one t'other. And, Squire, there's a little bunty chick runs around there, it's just a pet, and it makes its nest under a trundle bed where my little girl used to sleep til she got big enough to sleep up there with us. You know you can't sleep with them leastl'uns. You're liable to roll on 'em and clubfoot 'em.

"Well, she took her little cousin under that bed to see that nest. They's under there about a minute . . . no, it couldn't a-been a half a minute till the fight started. They fit, rolled over in the corner where them sills is weak and broke through the floor and damned if that big black hog of mine didn't bite both of 'em before I retch 'em up through there again. I set a keg over the hole and let 'em fight . . . little bits of things, couldn't hurt one t'other.

"Well, they fit around there about an hour. I looked over

and I saw my woman get red around the roots of her hair. Finally she raised up and said, 'Damned if I'm gonna raise no young'un of mine to get beat by no damn Spurlock!'

"And right there Sister Lockhoney flew red. She's got a heart in her six feet wide and four feet deep, she ain't a-feared of hell, she's a Medcalf. And before you could snap your fingers there's two couples on the floor and the house it a-rockin'. Well, they fit way on in to dusk. I kicked the fire up to get a light and I seen all four of 'em there agin that sewing machine I went up to Sears & Roebuck and got. I paid twenty-nine dollars and some odd cents fer it and packed it across the mountain, and I said to myself, Jesus Christ, they're fixing to ruin my instrument.

"I ris to my feet and never had no antipathy in my heart, I's just gonna separate 'em, that's all I's a-gonna do, take my machine and put it on the bed. And just as I got up Abner Spurlock, damned one-eyed son of a . . . he fit in the Yankee Army! . . . hit me the damndest pop, I seed stars. I just took out to the wood pile to get the axe, wasn't gone a second, Squire, I wasn't gone a half a second . . . don't you know he damned near had that fight over before I got back in there. Well, I took that axe and evened it up some, and Pap he heered a rumpus up on the mountain and come down there with his gun and peered in the window. His son and daughter both fighting one t'other, he didn't know which side fer to take, so he just backed off and he shot two shoots through there . . . aimed 'em low, never hurt nobody . . . barked up the children some. Then that half-witted brother of mine, he come in with a scythe, and you know Henry, by God, he'll keep any fight a-going.

"I said, 'Henry, keep that fight a-going til I go up on the mountain and see the Law.'

"Now, Squire, them's the facts in the case, as I go down that holler and whip them damned fellers or get myself a peace warrant."

Riley Wilson

Southern Humor:
The Light and the Dark

ROBERT J. HIGGS

I've collected lots of stuff on humor and sports—file cabinets full—and it reminds me of what someone said that the more you look at any subject, from a different angle, it becomes instantly more complex. This is certainly true of Appalachian humor. It has an element of trickery. I've been studying sports a long time, been interested in the humor of this region, and it crossed my mind some time ago that in all the years I've been in school, I've never heard anyone talk about tricks. Tricks are the essence of Nature. Nature plays tricks with animals in the fields. People play tricks on one another, and we legitimize tricks in sports. We like to see a good curved ball in baseball, but we don't like for anyone to throw us a curve off the field. Basketball is made up of tricks, as is boxing, etc.

Well, humor is a form of trickery, and it's legitimate. We announce when we are going to employ humor, and we give license to people to engage in trickery. There is a suddenness about it, there is a surprise, and there is a twist. One of my daughter's favorite jokes that is making the rounds at the University of Tennessee illustrates the twist or surprise:

A student goes complaining to the professor and wants to know why he made an "F." The professor says, "Because, young man, that is the lowest grade that this institution recognizes."

I want to recommend a great book: Arthur Koestler's *The Act of Creation*. In it, Koestler says there are three areas of creativity: humor, discovery and art. He uses the comic as the illustration for humor, science for discovery, and poetry for art. The essence of all of them is two planes, two things coming together. A simile is a comparison, and a metaphor relates two things of unlike nature. Science, among other things, is a comparison of two things. Who would have thought until Einstein came along that energy and mass were the same thing?

Now, this is what a joke is: a bi-association of thought at two levels. Koestler gives this example from Freud, who goes deeply into wit and its relationship to the unconscious. A man comes home one night and finds his wife in bed with a bishop. So he goes over to the window, doesn't say anything, but starts making ecclesiastical movements at the window. His wife says, "My dear, what are you doing?" And he says, "The bishop is performing my duty, so I'm performing his." (Koestler, p. 33) The point that Koestler makes here is that this is a discharge; it's a sudden surprise, a twist, a trick, and a catastrophe is averted. Koestler contrasts this with tragedy in Shakespeare's *Othello*. In the situation with the Bishop, the pent-up energy explodes and drains off immediately; in the case of the tragedy, it ebbs away in a gradual catharsis. In all instances, in art, in comedy, and in science, there is evidence of thinking. Koestler puts the jester, the sage, and the poet all on the same level. The comic has the element of the aggressive in it. This is one thing that distinguishes it from the scientific and the artistic. The jester is quite often the fool or the trickster, and he will appear even perverse sometimes, but he's always aggressive.

Now, there is a basic difference, as W.H. Auden points out, between satire and comedy. I think what we have in southern Appalachia is comedy, based upon this description by Auden in his introduction to *The Selected Prose of Byron* (p. xi):

> Satire attempts to show that the behavior of the individual or group within society violates the laws of ethics or common sense, on the assumption that once the majority are aware of the facts, they will become morally indignant and either compel the violators to mend their ways or render them socially and politically impotent. Comedy, on the other hand, is concerned with illusions, and self-deceptions, which all men indulge in, as to what they, and the world they live in are really like and cannot, so long as they remain human, help being. The object of comic exposure is not a special individual or a special group, but every man or every human society as a whole. Satire is angry and optimistic—it believes that the evil it attacks can be abolished; comedy is good-tempered and pessimistic—it believes that however much we may wish we could, we cannot change human nature and must make the best of a bad job.

So the main point I would make about Appalachian humor is that it is full of tricks. It revels in language and it is comic rather than satiric.

I don't think that there is a more important subject than humor. Konrad Lorenz says that humor and knowledge are the two great hopes of mankind (Lorenz, p. 288). We don't take humor seriously enough. In his book *Gods and Games*, David Miller says that back at the time of Plato and Aristotle, seriousness won out over humor and that ever since, we have been serious about nationalism, we've been serious about religion, and this is why history has taken the course that it has (Miller, pp. 107–8). People have not laughed very much compared to the blood they've shed. They've not been very tolerant.

Play is at the opposite end of seriousness. The middle way is dealt with by Hugo Rahner in a book, *Man at Play*, using the term *eutrapelia*. Rahner points out that *eutra-pelos* means the well-turning man (Rahner, p. 100). On one side is something serious, and on the other something playful, and the really wise, sane, intelligent, good man is able to turn from one to the other with relative ease and without being hung up and strung out. He's the well-turning man. Now, it's not a fusion of categories. The Church saw that as a type of heresy. Play and religion are separate. Appalachian writers and tellers of tales would never have thought that play and religion are the same thing. Categories remain distinct, and that's an important point which allows us to look at religion in a serious way and the rest of life in a comic way. Worship is a separate category from play, and they should not be confused. I think that distinction has been retained carefully in Appalachian comedy and writing, and it reflects a Calvinistic point of view. It is a credit to the wisdom of the people in that regard. They haven't fallen into the error of mixing the two. Let me cite three good examples of *eutrapelos*. One is Dr. Samuel Johnson. He and Boswell were out walking in the country one day and Dr. Johnson handed Boswell his coat and rolled down the hill, as Heywood Hale Broun said, "like a great laughing brown ball," but arose at the bottom "hay-streaked and refreshed." This is the man who gave us the *Dictionary of the English Language*.

Another is Henry David Thoreau, who was walking in the woods one day and saw a fox and set out to chase him. It is a marvelous thing to read about Thoreau chasing that fox.

Also in Loren Eisley's *The Unexpected Universe*, there is this wonderful story of how Eisley is out walking on the beach one day when he sees a little fox near a shipwreck. He goes over there and looks down at the fox, and guess what the fox does? He picks up a chicken bone and shakes it at Eisley, wanting to play. So Eisley gets a larger chicken bone, puts it in his mouth, and gets down on all fours with the fox, and he describes it: "There was a universe opened to me. I've had my one miracle of life. It was a laughing universe, a tiny universe. It was a side of the universe of play." (Eisley, p. 210) There is that playful element in the universe, but there is also in Eisley's account an element of worship. This was a man who could turn from science to a playful attitude. This playful attitude has been one of the characteristics of the literature of this region.

These incidents are examples of *eutrapelia,* the middle way that allows one to turn from one way of seeing things to another.

I want to mention another book, *American Humor* by Constance Rourke. The humor of America, she says, comes from three main sources. It comes from the New England Yankee; it comes from the backwoodsman, that is, the frontiersman from Kentucky, Tennessee, Arkansas, people from all of these places; and from Negro minstrelsy. These three traditions came together and merged into the tall tale, the trademark of American humor.

The tale, Rourke says, is absolutely infectious, and some great people could not resist it. Here is what she said about J.J. Audubon (Rourke, p. 50):

> Audubon, for example, glided easily into this tradition, always the backwoodsman, the wanderer, a prime shot. His massive achievement in painting the birds of America—"my beloved birds"—in their native habitat was an enlarged reflection of an expert huntsman's knowledge. He joined in the merry-making of the backwoods and played the fiddle and the flageolet. He had the western gift for opulent self-portraiture. He loved costume and was inordinately proud of his long thick hair, and appeared in London in later years garbed in green and crimson. He loved disguise and once on a journey dressed . . . like a French seaman, and thereafter insisted that he had grown up at sea. When Rafinesque, the eccentric naturalist, appeared in Kentucky, Audubon invented and described to him wholly unknown species of birds; for information as to the fishes of Ohio, Audubon drew upon rivers of an abundant fantasy and pictured fishes of such colors and strange shapes, such amaz-

ing habits and exploits, that they might have belonged to another world. Among them were the Devil-Jack Diamond-Fish that grew to be ten feet in length and was armored with large stone scales of diamond shapes, set in oblique rows, which were bulletproof, and which when dried would strike fire with steel.

Rafinesque was also a romantic and afterwards engaged in the scheme to induce mussels of the Ohio River to make pearls: he should have capped Audubon's stories. But he let himself gaze at the flinty fish at a distance and afterwards declared that he had seen one of its scales. He accepted all of these stories and was plunged into long and cumbersome toil in consequence and suffered discredit as a scientist. Entranced, he even followed Audubon on a bear-hunt and was led a wild chase through densest canebrakes where fire suddenly lent fury to the scene, with water in the jointed stalks exploding like shells and suggesting the advance of Indians with musketry. A bear lunged out, thunder broke and rain fell. Rafinesque, attempting to flee, became hopelessly jammed. The only mode of exit was to crawl, and such travel had terrors, for the canebrake was haunted by serpents and panthers and bears.

British scientists proclaimed Audubon a new and greater Baron Munchausen. "Sir," said one, "this is really too much even for us Englishmen to swallow, whose gullets are known to be the largest, the widest and the most elastic in the world." (Rourke, pp. 51–52) Scientists themselves, in the case of Audubon, could not escape the tendency to tell the tall tale.

The main element of mountain humor is the trick. It revels in language. It is comic as opposed to satiric. It is not deceived by human nature. The essence to mountain humor is like coal. It is deep, it is dark and it is hard. It is ironic. It is aware of the difference between man as he is and a better state, and it points to this difference. Deep

South humor is essentially sentimental. It is light, like cotton, fluffy, worn where you can see it. It is on the surface. It is easy to commercialize. It appears on the Grand Ole Opry.

Let us think of two men named Harris. One was George Washington Harris, who wrote *Sut Lovingood Yarns*, about a Tennessee mountaineer. The other is Joel Chandler Harris, who wrote the stories about Uncle Remus and his animal friends. Uncle Remus's world is an Edenic place. It is sentimental. Everything is hunky-dory. This is what we read to our children. It is instructional and educational. But we do not read the Sut Lovingood yarns to our children because we think them too coarse and brutal, and unfortunately many people go through life without having read them. They show man to be, in essence, a sinful creature, a dark mysterious creature. Consider this statement from Sut Lovingood, for example (Harris, pp. 174–75):

> Whar there ain't enough feed, big childer roots little childer outen the troff, and gobbils up thar part. Jis' so the yeath over: the bishops eats the elders, the elders eats common peopil, they eats such cattil as me, I eats possums, possums eats chickins, chickins swallers wums, wums am content to eat dus, and dus am the aind of hit all.

Now, you won't hear that on the Ole Opry! That is about as dark a humor as you can get, almost as dark as Shakespeare's "tomorrow and tomorrow and tomorrow." It is reminiscent of Swift, and it is like the dark Twain. Twain loved Sut, and Faulkner did, and Wolfe loved this kind of humor too. This is the dark side of Appalachian literature and humor, but I suggest to you that in a world where at any minute whole cities could be obliterated, we should not be offended by language that might indeed point out our own sinful nature and shortcomings. I am reminded of that famous line from Flannery O'Connor's "A Good Man Is Hard to Find," where The Misfit says, "She would of been a good woman if it had been somebody there to

shoot her every minute of her life." To me, that is the type
of wisdom that comes out of the mountains. It is ironic
humor, and it is deep and dark. We'd be pretty good people
if there were somebody there to shoot us every minute of
our lives.

I want to close with a quote from Mark Twain's *Autobiography* (p. 298):

> There are those who say that a novel should be a
> work of art solely and you must not preach in it. You
> must not teach in it. That may be true in regard to
> novels, but it is not true in regard to humor. Humor
> must not professedly teach, and it must not pro-
> fessedly preach, but it must do both if it is to live
> forever.

I think that is what the humor of George Washington
Harris does, and that is what the best humor of the mountains does. It causes us to think about our dark and mysterious nature.

Auden, W. H. *Introduction to the Selected Poetry and Prose of Byron*. New York: New American Library, 1966.

Eisley, Loren. *The Unexpected Universe*. New York: Harcourt Brace Jovanovich, 1969.

Harris, George Washington. *Sut Lovingood Yarns,* ed. M. Thomas Inge. New Haven: College and University Press, 1966.

Koestler, Arthur. *Act of Creation*. New York: McMillan Co., 1964.

Lorenz, Konrad. *On Aggression*. New York: Bantam Books, 1971.

Miller, David. *Gods and Games*. New York: World, 1970.

Rahner, Hugo, *Man at Play*. New York: Herder and Herder, 1972.

Rourke, Constance. *American Humor: A Study of the National Character*. Garden City, N.Y.: Doubleday, 1953.

Twain, Mark. *The Autobiography of Mark Twain,* ed. Charles Neider. New York: Washington Square Press, 1961.